THE ART OF MAKING FINE

WOOD JEWELRY

THE ART OF MAKING FINE

WOOD JEWELRY

Tony Lydgate

Sterling Publishing Co. Inc., New York
A Sterling/Chapelle Book

Chapelle Ltd.
Owner:
Jo Packham

Design/Layout Editor:
Gerry De Soto

Staff:
Marie Barber, Ann Bear, Areta Bingham, Kass Burchett, Rebecca Christensen, Holly Fuller, Marilyn Goff, Shirley Heslop, Holly Hollingsworth, Shawn Hsu, Susan Jorgensen, Pauline Locke, Ginger Mikkelsen, Barbara Milburn, Linda Orton, Karmen Quinney, Rhonda Rainey, Leslie Ridenour, and Cindy Stoeckl

Photography:
Kevin Dilley, photographer for Hazen Photography

Photo Stylist:
Leslie Liechty

Drawings:
Richard Long

Library of Congress Cataloging-in-Publication Data
Available

If you have any questions or comments or would like information about any specialty products featured in this book, please contact:

A Sterling/Chapelle Book

Published by Sterling Publishing Company, Inc.
387 Park Avenue South, New York, NY 10016
© 1998 by Chapelle Ltd.
Distributed in Canada by Sterling Publishing
c/o Canadian Manda Group,
One Atlantic Avenue, Suite 105
Toronto, Ontario, Canada M6K 3E7
Distributed in Great Britain and Europe by Cassell PLC
Wellington House, 125 Strand,
London WC2R 0BB, England
Distributed in Australia by Capricorn Link
(Australia) Pty Ltd.
P.O. Box 6651, Baulkham Hills, Business Centre, NSW
2153, Australia
Printed in China
All Rights Reserved

Sterling ISBN 0-8069-0361-9

Chapelle Ltd., Inc.
P.O. Box 9252
Ogden, UT 84409

Phone: (801) 621-2777
FAX: (801) 621-2788

CONTENTS

Photo by Judy Dater

My love of wood has its roots on islands in the Pacific and Atlantic Oceans. My family is originally from the Hawaiian Island of Kauai, where Lydgate State Park is named after my grandfather, and I grew up surrounded by the fabulous color, texture and smell of woods such as koa, mango, milo, ohia and sandalwood. As a young man transported to Martha's Vineyard, off the coast of New England, I had the great good fortune to be apprenticed to a Master Builder engaged in restoring Eighteenth Century whaling captains' homes. These were constructed by shipwrights, many without the use of nails or other metal fasteners. I was awed by what these builders' hands had accomplished, and determined to discover what mine might do.

I turned to woodwork full-time in 1978, and over the years my functional jewelry boxes and sculptural chests have appeared in art galleries, fine woodworking stores, and juried craft exhibitions throughout the country. I am a firm believer in the importance of giving away what I know, which has led to the many articles I have published on both the art and the business of woodwork. Seventh in a series of books I have written for Chapelle/Sterling, *The Art of Making Fine Wood Jewelry* has two aims: to celebrate the brilliant work of our contemporary American woodworkers, and to tell something about not only how, but why people like you make beautiful things.

Jewelry is an appealing project for woodworkers of any skill level, from beginner to expert, because it is small, low in materials expense, and can be made with nothing more than simple hand tools. Unlike boxes or furniture, which often require costly quantities of lumber and a large shop well-equipped with power tools, the wood jewelry maker's output is affordable, manageable, and portable.

In addition to these practical advantages, there is an aesthetic advantage as well, for wood jewelry distills the essence of woodworking into its most concentrated form. Nothing is better than jewelry at showing off the effects woodworkers strive for: the liquid sheen of a brilliantly polished hardwood surface; precise, intricate forms, whose gracefulness disguises the complex techniques by which they were fabricated; and the bright figure of naturally colorful wood flashing in the light.

To explore the pleasures of personal adornments made of wood, this book presents a treasury of designs by twenty-four of the country's leading woodworkers. Complete with exploded diagrams and complete how-to building instructions, these include earrings, brooches and pins, bracelets, pendants, necklaces, combs, bolo ties - even wooden clutch purses that are themselves works of art. Some of the projects are entirely wood, others combine wood with traditional jewelry materials such as silver and semiprecious stones. All are designed to be made in the home workshop, and are intended solely for personal use, and not for commercial manufacture or sale.

Because of its small size, wood jewelry tends to rely more on hand tools than do larger woodworking projects. Some operations, however, such as preparing hardwood stock to be milled into the laminates and workpieces that will eventually become jewelry, may be performed more quickly using the following common power tools.

NOTE: When using power tools, always wear eye and ear protection. For important information about operating a safe shop, please read the section on Safety, on page 15.

POWER TOOLS

TABLESAW

This basic shop tool will rip, crosscut, and resaw stock up to about 6" wide. A 10" blade diameter is the most practical, and heavier-duty models are preferable because they are more accurate, especially for repeated cuts. A sturdy fence, which can be used on either side of the sawblade, and an adjustable miter fence are essential accessories. Sawblades should be carbide tipped, and kept as sharp as possible. For the fine cutting needed in jewelry making, select an 80-tooth or finer blade. Blades accumulate resin, especially when milling dense hardwoods; after each hour of use, clean them with spray-on oven cleaner.

BELT SANDER

Sanding objects with flat surfaces is easiest on a stationary belt sander. Hand-held 4" x 24" models may be adapted for workbench use by turning them belt-side up, then attaching them firmly in a shop-built carrier clamped to the bench. A larger size, 6" x 48", is available as a freestanding tool, often including a 9" or 12" sanding disc. On this larger size model, the idler cylinder (the one not attached to the motor), usually about 3" in diameter, can serve as a drumsander.

DRILLPRESS

A freestanding or bench model of this tool is essential for accurate drilling of fine holes in jewelry stock. The drillpress can also be made into a sanding tool, using sanding drum attachments, available in a variety of rigid and flexible sizes.

BANDSAW

With a wide blade, the bandsaw is useful for resawing lumber. When fitted with progressively narrower and finer-toothed blades, the bandsaw is the tool of choice for many rough shaping operations. It is also used for slicing strips off laminate blocks. To ensure greatest accuracy, a circular table insert can be made from hardboard, and replaced whenever the blade has widened its slot.

LATHE

Some of the jewelry projects in this book, such as Judy Ditmer's pins and earrings, page 86, and Bonnie Klein's bolo ties and Baseball necklace, page 132, require the use of a woodturner's lathe. Since a complete description of the lathe is beyond the scope of this book, consult the Sterling/Chapelle book *The Art of the Lathe* by Patrick Spielman.

JOINER

During the early stages of a jewelry project, this tool is useful for creating a flat face on lumber stock, as well as for removing rough surfaces.

THICKNESS SANDER

Although not all home shops have this tool, most mills and many cabinet shops do. Especially when making more than one project, it can be worth the effort to gain access to a thickness sander, because it saves so much time in cleaning up surfaces, as well as in producing precisely dimensioned thicknesses.

JIGSAW or SCROLL SAW

Even with a fine-tooth blade, the bandsaw is often too coarse a tool for the cuts needed in jewelry making, as in the intricate brooches and necklaces by Dawn Nelson and William Harris on page 139. For such fine work, the appropriate tool is a bench-mounted jigsaw or scroll saw. For a complete description of techniques, consult *The Art of the Scroll Saw* by Patrick Spielman, published by Sterling/Chapelle.

DRUM SANDER

Available in a variety of sizes as a bench tool, or as an attachment to a drillpress or bench shaft, drum sanders can be fitted with abrasive-covered cylinders in diameters ranging from 1/2" to 6". Inflatable cylinders are also available for shaping irregular curved surfaces.

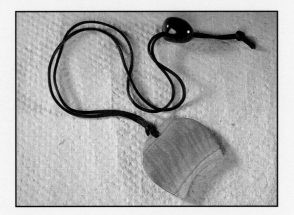

HAND TOOLS

CARVING KNIVES

Many of the projects in this book, such as Karen Scates's miniatures on page 44, or Tom Allen's brooches on page 97, are carved with gouges, a utility knife, or surgical scalpel. Cutters of various types are available from woodworking specialty stores and mail-order catalogs: experiment with different sizes and shapes to find the ones that best fit your hand and your project.

FILES, RASPS, RIFFLERS

Removing excess material from wood surfaces is often best done with one of these metal abrasive tools, also available in a large variety of sizes and shapes from woodworking specialty stores and mail-order catalogs.

PAPER CUTTER

As an alternative to a knife and straight edge, thin strips of wood such as veneers may be cut to size using a guillotine-type paper cutter with a good quality blade.

MAGNIFYING GLASSES, or MAGNIFYING VISOR

A magnifying glass or visor can assist visual inspection of small scale and detailed work.

FLEXIBLE SHAFT TOOL

Woodworking, dental, and jewelry supply manufacturers all produce a version of this hand held electric tool, to which fine tips such as rasps, drills, sawblades, and abrasives can be attached.

JEWELERS' TOOLS

Several of the artists featured in this book, such as Carol Windsor (page 135), were jewelers before they became woodworkers. Jewelers' tools are similar to many woodworking tools, but since they are designed for metal, they are capable of maintaining more precise tolerances.

STRONG LIGHTING

Close work and fine detail require appropriate lighting. Depending on their individual preferences, the woodworkers in this book use a combination of fluorescent, incandescent, and halogen lighting, in addition to natural daylight. Experiment with the light source that best fits your working environment.

ADHESIVES

Aliphatic or "white" glue, a convenient and economical adhesive, is appropriate for most projects. Two-part epoxy, urethane, cyanoacrylate, and various types of waterproof glue may also be used. Be sure to wear protective gloves and to follow manufacturer's instructions. Glue should completely cover surfaces to be joined, and in general, too much glue is preferable to too little: a slight squeeze of excess is evidence that there is sufficient glue to hold securely.

CREATIVE TECHNIQUES AND DESIGN

As every woodworker knows, there are many different ways to perform any given operation, and readers are encouraged to adapt their own tools and techniques. Exploring new ways of doing something often leads to alternative techniques, novel designs, and discoveries. In the perfectly equipped shop, where machines do all the thinking, such discoveries are rarely encountered.

Another source of innovation is the errors that even the most skilled craftsman will inevitably make. A number of the designs in this book, including some by Buzz Coren (page 71) and by Walter and Nora Bennett (page 17), for example, began as mistakes. Look at mistakes not as annoying obstacles, but rather as a creative opportunity, one that allows you to view your design from a new perspective.

JEWELRY FINDINGS

The fasteners by which jewelry is attached to clothing or to the body are known as findings. These include metal clasps, hooks, wires, posts, clips, rings, pins, and chains, as well as cords of silk, wire, leather, silver, and gold.

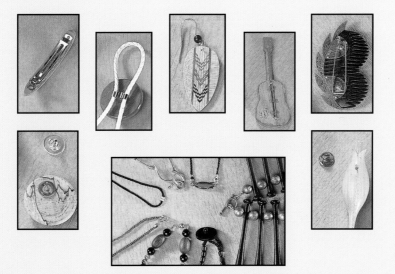

Findings are available from mail-order catalogs in a wide variety of sizes, shapes, grades, and styles, and are easily assembled into your jewelry project, usually with nothing more complicated than an appropriate adhesive.

SELECTING LUMBER

Much of the visual impact of the jewelry in this book comes from the natural beauty of wood, and each project includes a listing of the woods used. Highly figured hardwood is especially appropriate for jewelry; it results from natural irregularities and deformities, as do pearls and many gemstones.

   Wood jewelry offers the perfect opportunity to utilize small pieces of wood that are colored, shaped, figured, or even deformed in interesting ways. Such pieces can often be found lying around the woodshop; they have been saved from the firewood pile or the scrap bin – sometimes for years – because although too small to use, they are too nice to throw away. While the jewelry projects in this book utilize some imported species, many designs feature native North American woods such as ash, elm, hickory, sycamore, maple, walnut, hop hornbeam, oak, bodark,
dogwood, apple, pear, and other fruitwoods. Attractive grain patterns and defects such as burl, birdseye, crotch, curly or fiddleback, and spalting often appear in these species. Sources for such woods include your own and your neighbor's backyard, the highway department, tree trimming companies, even the local dump. When purchasing lumber from a dealer or lumberyard, be certain any hardwoods you buy are certified to come from a source that practices sustainable yield forest management.
   One of the most useful products for making jewelry is wood veneer, the general name given to thin slices of solid wood. In stock at some hardwood lumberyards, and widely available by mail-order from woodworking catalogs, veneer comes in a large variety of species, in thicknesses of approximately 1/32". In addition, many suppliers offer veneers made from hardwoods that are dyed in a broad palette of colors. The bright, unnatural greens, reds, yellows, and blues of these artificially dyed veneers can be used by themselves, or combined with naturally colored hardwood for dramatic visual effect.

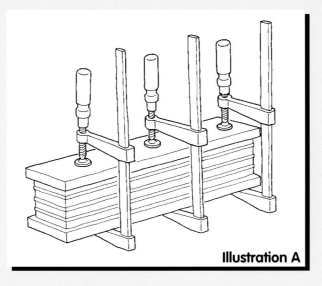

Illustration A

LAMINATES

Some of the jewelry projects in this book are created from laminates, a series of thin strips of solid wood glued together to form a striped block. Once made, this laminate block can then be resawn to produce fascinating patterns, as illustrated in designs such as those of David Marson (pages 58-61). To make a laminate, follow this basic procedure, shown in **Illustrations A and B**.

• Prepare stock in differing woods to be milled into laminate strips. The width and hthickness of the stock will depend on the desired dimensions of the finished laminate. The length of the stock should be a minimum of 10", as shorter lengths are awkward to rip on the bandsaw or tablesaw. Store-bought veneer may be used in a laminate without prior milling, unless its thickness is noticeably irregular.

• Using a pushstick, rip the stock into laminate strips of the desired thickness. When using a tablesaw for ripping, strips with thicknesses greater than 1/8" may be ripped between the blade and the fence. For thicknesses less than 1/8", it is advisable to place the bulk of the workpiece between the blade and fence, and have the laminate strip come off the workpiece to the left of the blade.

• Mill two sandwich blocks from plywood or scrap lumber 1/2" to 3/4" in thickness, and the same length and width as the laminate strips. These sandwich blocks serve to spread the force of the clamping evenly throughout the laminate assembly.

• Make a dry assembly of the laminate, without glue, to make certain all surfaces are flat and all strips are properly milled.

• Apply adhesive to one face of each strip of the laminate and assemble. True up the edges of the assembly, then add the sandwich blocks, and position the clamps. Tighten the clamps slowly, being certain that none of the strips skids out, and that the assembly stays rectangular.

• When the assembly is dry, mill its vertical edges on the tablesaw, bandsaw, or sanding disc to remove excess glue, and to restore 90-degree angles to the laminate block. Use the tablesaw or bandsaw, as shown in Illustration B, to resaw the laminate block into new laminate strips, which can then be recombined to produce more complex designs. This re-combining process is shown in detail in the projects on pages 19-23.

13

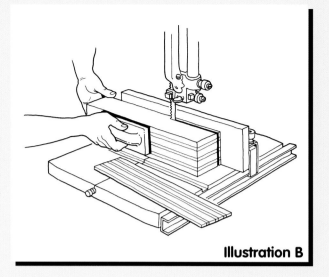

Illustration B

SANDING AND FINISHING

One of the most important elements in the look of a finished piece of jewelry is the shape and feel of its finished surfaces, and sanding is the operation that produces them. For designs that are sculpted out of a block of solid wood, like those of Bill Chappelow (page 90), the entire process, from rough shaping of the bandsawed block to final sanding and polishing, may be performed on the same belt or drum sander. Start with a coarse grit abrasive such as 60x, then progress in gradual stages to finer and finer grits.

Many jewelry makers prefer to do all their sanding and polishing by hand. Karen Scates (page 44) likes the feel of working the piece with her fingers: she sands with small bits of abrasive paper that she backs by attaching them to cutup sections of gum eraser. Fine sandpaper (300 to 600 grit), files, and steel wool may also be used in the last stages of smoothing.

For a particularly fine polish, many woodworkers use jeweler's rouge, available from woodworking specialty stores and mail-order catalogs. Jeweler's rouge is a paste product that contains an extremely fine abrasive grit.

Three general types of clear finish are used on the jewelry in this book, either independently or in combination: penetrating oil, which soaks into the wood and then hardens; shellac, lacquer or varnish, which lie on top of it; and wax.

Penetrating or 'hand-rubbed' oil finishes show off dramatic figure and grain patterns better than lacquer or varnish, whose multiple coats covering the surface tend to fill the pores of the wood. Oil finishes are relatively simple to apply, and have the advantage of not requiring a dust-free environment. Oil can be applied with a cloth, and rubbed in with fine steel wool. When the surface is dry, steel wool is again used to smooth it. The final step is to apply an appropriate wax, which is then rubbed to high lustre by hand or with a buffing wheel. Some designers, such as Sharon Whitmore (page 99), dispense with oil altogether, and finish solely with wax.

Other wood jewelry makers prefer shellac, lacquer, varnish, or polyurethane coatings.

In both brush-on and spray cans, these are available in either water-based or oil-based formulations. The water-based versions may raise the grain when applied, and can necessitate sanding between coats.

Because jewelry comes in close contact with the wearer's skin, check manufacturer's specifications for any finishing product to make certain it is not chemically reactive after drying.

SAFETY

Woodworking is inherently dangerous. The raw material itself can be heavy, sharp-edged, and splintery. The tools used to fabricate it are potentially lethal. These factors, combined with noxious dust, harmful chemicals, high noise levels, and large quantities of electricity, produce an environment in which disfiguring, crippling, or even fatal injury can occur in dozens of unforeseen ways. To operate a safe workshop, always keep this in mind.

The risk of injury can never be completely removed, but it can be reduced to an acceptable level by strict observation of certain guidelines.

• For safe operation of all tools, fully understand and adhere to the manufacture's instructions.

• Never allow fingers to come near any moving blade or cutter. Use a push stick.

• Always wear a respirator or dust mask in the shop. Always wear ear and eye protection when using power tools.

• Always wear appropriate clothing. A heavy work apron will protect the midsection from the occasional table saw kickback. A dropped chisel hurts less on a protected toe than on a bare one—do not wear sandals in the shop.

• Never perform any operation without being satisfied that you understand it and are comfortable with it.

• Keep your mind on your work. Do not allow your attention to wander, especially when performing any repetitive operations.

• Never work when tired, in a hurry, or simply not in the mood to work. It is better to stop, or find something to do outside the shop for a while. Return refreshed and in the proper frame of mind.

Photo by DP Photos

WALTER AND NORA BENNETT

While pursuing their careers as mental health professionals, Walter and Nora Bennett found themselves increasingly interested in woodwork. As the couple's explorations in wood progressed through boxmaking, Nora kept noticing how jewellike their small boxes looked. "We were using laminated busy-block patterns in some of our pieces," recalls Nora. "I've always enjoyed marquetry, and as I began to play around with veneers, we just gradually evolved into making jewelry.

"The biggest single thing that changed the look of our work was when we began using dyed veneers. These give you so much more versatility, and combining the dyed colors with natural woods creates endless variations. Interestingly, some of our best designs began as mistakes. There's nothing like a good mistake to break you out of your set mold of thinking and help you see things from a fresh point of view."

In their Pennsylvania studio, Walter and Nora produce boxes and clocks as well as jewelry. One of Nora's favorite things about the business is finding out how to engineer so many parts into a small object. "You need very accurate cuts, and the right amount of pressure in the right places. It's really fun to figure out how to make something for which there really aren't regular tools."

The Bennetts use a wide variety of hardwoods and hardwood veneers for their jewelry, including oak, maple, butternut, mahogany, walnut, ash, cherry, red cedar, and chakte cok, as well as dyed veneers.

SQUARE AND PINWHEEL EARRINGS

• Following the instructions for laminates on page 13, mill and glue a laminate rod 1/4" x 1/2" x 10", as shown in illustration **Bennett 1**. The pinwheel earrings in the photograph on page 16 consist of a two-part laminate, with a square block in the center of each earring; the drawing **Bennett 3** shows the outline for this design with a three-part laminate.

• Crosscut the laminate rod into segments 1" long. Assemble four segments into the pinwheel pattern, measure the interior square, and mill a block of contrasting wood to fit.
Glue the assembly.

• Sand and polish. Apply a wash coat of shellac, followed by polyurethane. Glue on an earring back.

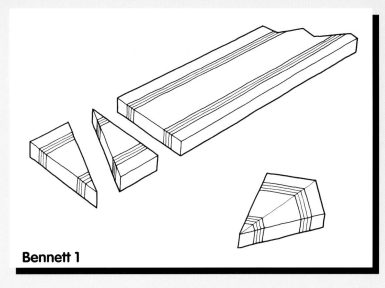

Bennett 1

KITE EARRINGS

• Mill and glue 10" long laminate rods of contrasting wood strips of various widths, from 1/32" to 1/2", as shown in illustrations **Bennett 1** and **Bennett 2**. Natural or dyed veneer may be used for the narrowest strips. All strips are 1/4" in thickness and a minimum of 10" long.

• Using the bandsaw, mill triangles from the resulting laminate, and glue to form the kite shape.

• Sand and polish. Apply a wash coat of shellac, followed by polyurethane. Glue on an earring back.

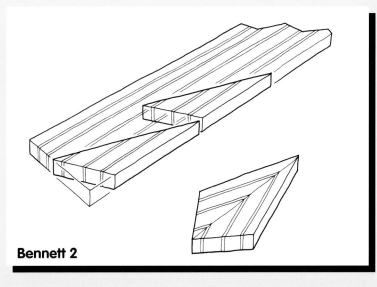

Bennett 2

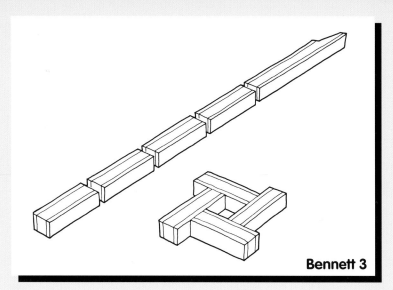

Bennett 3

STEPPED TEARDROP EARRINGS

• Use the laminate technique to make a laminate block with an interesting combination of woods.

• Using the bandsaw, mill a series of triangles, approximately 1/4" wide at the base, as shown in Illustration **Bennett 4**. Glue the triangles together, staggering them slightly.

• Drill a 1/16" diameter hole as close to the top of the earring as practical.

• Sand and polish. Apply a wash coat of shellac, followed by polyurethane.

• Attach earring wires.

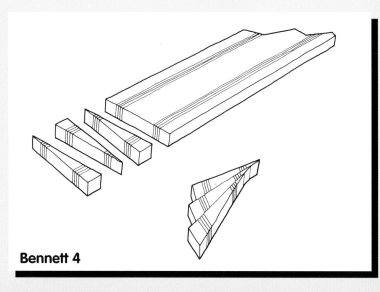

Bennett 4

WEDGE EARRINGS

• These intricate designs combine re-sawn laminates with solid wedges of contrasting woods. Start by preparing a 1/4" thick laminate rod, 10" long and 1" to 2" wide, such as the one shown in Illustration **Bennett 5-A**.

• When the laminate is dry, crosscut into strips each 3/16" wide.

• As shown in Illustration **Bennet 5-B**, reglue the strips into a new assembly, staggering them by about 1/2 ". When dry, trim the long edges of the laminate on the bandsaw or tablesaw.

• Bandsaw the laminate into triangles.

• To create earrings in which the wedges are separated from the laminate triangles by a contrasting wood border, glue the endgrain edges of the triangles to a 1/16" thick strip of ebony (illustration **Bennett 5-C**). Crosscut the triangles and the wedges, and then reassemble to create the final design.

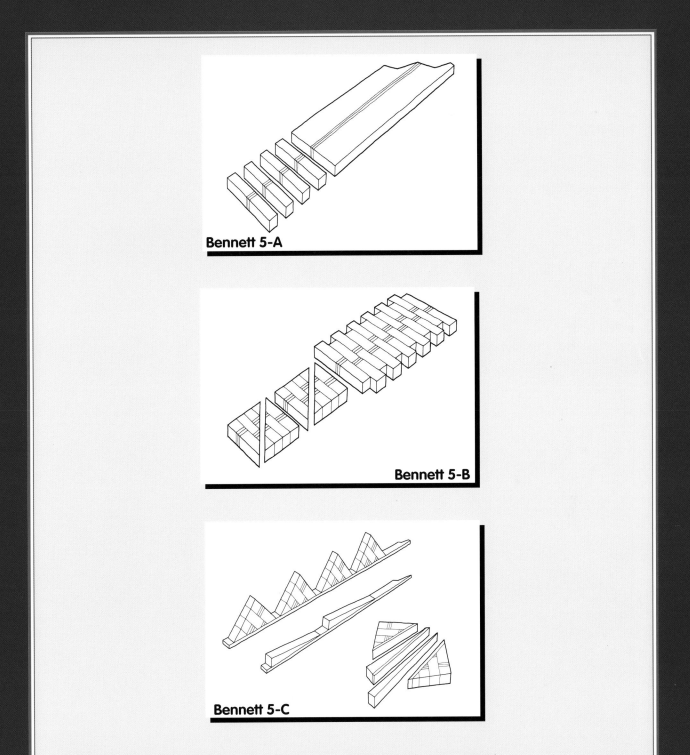

Bennett 5-A

Bennett 5-B

Bennett 5-C

- Drill a 1/16" diameter hole as close to the top of the earring as practical.
- Sand and polish. Apply a wash coat of shellac, followed by polyurethane.
- Attach earring wires.

KATHY FRANDEEN

Born in California, Kathy Frandeen prefers the natural coastal mountain surroundings of her home on the Pacific ocean north of Monterrey, where wilderness camping, hiking, tracking, and mountain biking provide the setting and inspiration for much of her work. She has given the name "thru-lay" to her technique for creating these unique hardwood feathers, which use solid woods in such a way that the design is visible on both sides of the piece.

"I made the first feather as a gift for a friend," Kathy says, "but I really came to woodworking through the back door. I started out working on boats, varnishing and refinishing, and doing house carpentry. I found that I loved wood, and when I had an opportunity to handcraft a set of dovetailed oak and teak doors, I said to myself, 'this is starting to feel more like it.'

"I've always been attracted to feathers, my house is filled with them today. Their shapes always seem to be changing, even though they stay the same. I continue to make furniture, particularly tables, but I like small things, so I find myself always evolving back to the feathers, which I can do by myself with just my two hands."

Kathy's feather pendants, earrings, necklaces and pins are made from natural sycamore, walnut, maple, ebony, koa, rosewood, pernambuco, lacewood, wenge, narra, and cocobolo, all with a hand-rubbed tung oil finish. Some are attached to their metal findings with waxed linen thread.

• The grain on either side of the central shaft of these wood feathers is angled, just like the avian feathers on which they are based. To create this effect, prepare a solid hardwood workpiece, 5/16" x 6" x 10". As shown in Illustration **Frandeen 1**, crosscut at an angle to make sections about 1" wide.

• From a contrasting wood, prepare another piece with similar dimensions. This will become the shaft of the feather. As shown in Illustration **Frandeen 2**, stack the two parts. Tape them together with masking tape, and draw the slightly curved outline of the left-hand edge of the feather shaft, shown as a dotted line in the drawing.

• Bandsaw the assembly along the dotted line. Remove the tape, separate the two parts, and glue them together. The result is shown in Illustration **Frandeen 3**.

• Select another section from the original hardwood workpiece, and set it underneath the result of the previous step, making certain that the grains of the two parts run in opposite directions.

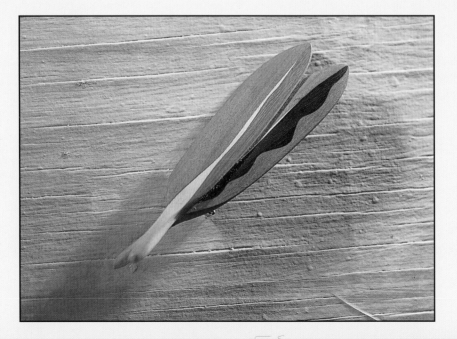

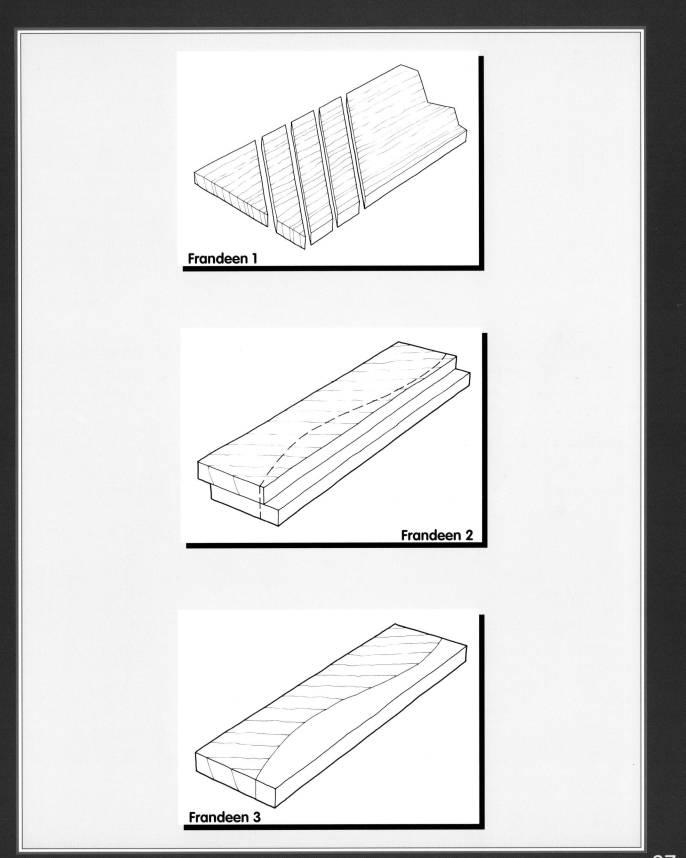

Frandeen 1

Frandeen 2

Frandeen 3

27

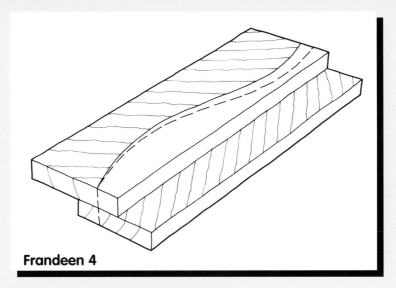

Frandeen 4

• Tape the parts together, draw the outline of the complete shaft, and bandsaw along the dotted line as shown in Illustration **Frandeen 4**.

• Glue the right-hand portion of the lower section to the left-hand portion of the upper section as shown in Illustration **Frandeen 5**. Draw the outline of the completed feather and bandsaw, producing the result shown in Illustration **Frandeen 6**.

• Sand the feather to final shape and polish. Drill a 1/16" diameter hole in the base of the shaft.

• Apply a hand-rubbed tung oil finish. When dry, attach appropriate cord or finding.

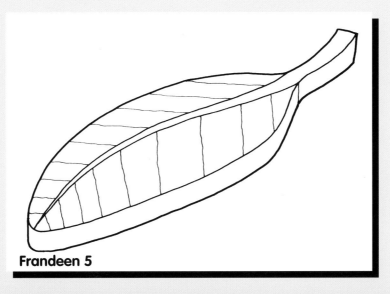

Frandeen 5

Photo by Chris Eaton

MARK BURHANS

To learn how to build from the ground up, Mark Burhans interrupted his college studies in architecture to gain firsthand experience by becoming a carpenter and cabinetmaker. Only when he felt he had mastered these practical skills did he return to school to complete a Bachelor of Fine Arts degree in woodworking and furniture making.

Among the master woodworkers he encountered during his schooling, he was most impressed by the woodturners. "I liked the lathe," Mark says, "because it was the only woodworking tool I knew of where you could go from raw wood to finished piece on one machine."

As Mark explored forms on the lathe, he began to develop his distinctive vases and pins, all based on the tulip shape. "I try to give each piece an organic

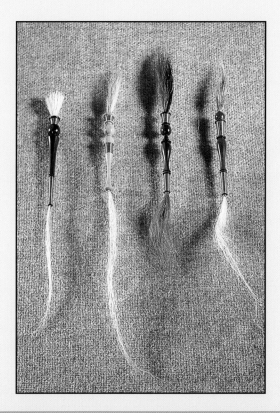

quality which, like ripe fruit, seems to radiate life from within." Now based in Ohio, he also turns "Whispering Spirit" pins. "You know that moment you sometimes have in a half-dream state, when suddenly everything seems incredibly clear and lucid, and the next moment, it's gone? These pins are my attempt to describe that moment in a form."

The earrings and flower vase pins are made from small pieces of maple, elm, hickory, beech or sycamore with a dramatic pattern of swirling black lines called spalting. Caused by a fungus, spalting sometimes develops in fallen timber that has been exposed to moisture. Spalted wood can be found at selected lumber dealers, in the firewood pile, and occasionally on the forest floor.

• To make the earrings, select a block of spalted wood 1-1/8" square and 1/4" thick. Mount on the lathe and turn to a round shape with a slightly domed profile. Fine sand and apply shellac to the workpiece while still on the lathe. Remove from the lathe and apply a buffed wax finish. Glue on earring backs.

• Wildflower pins are designed to hold a live flower, its stem inserted with a small quantity of moisture into a glass tube inside the wood. They are turned from 3-1/2" lengths of 3/4" spalted turning squares. Fine sand and apply shellac to the workpiece while still on the lathe. Remove from the lathe and drill a 1/4" diameter hole 1-3/4" deep in the petal end. Insert a 1/4" x 2" glass tube. Glue on a pin back, then apply a buffed wax finish.

• The "Whispering Spirit" pins are turned from 3" lengths of 1/4" turning squares in maple, walnut, and ebony. Fine sand and apply shellac to the workpiece while still on the lathe. Remove from the lathe and apply a buffed wax finish. Wrap sections of the turning with copper, brass, gold, or silver wire. Drill both ends and the central area with a 1/32" drill bit. Insert horsehair and pin back.

PATRICK LEONARD

Work smarter, not harder" has always been Patrick Leonard's motto. Like all woodworkers, however, he faces a familiar dilemma: how to meet the economic needs of his Pennsylvania-based business and family, without losing the sheer enjoyment and personal fulfillment of making beautiful things.

"When I was twelve, my Mom and I put a workshop in the back of the trailer we were living in," Patrick remembers. "My only tools then were a Sears circular saw and a hammer, but I made a pine 5-drawer nightstand as a gift for my Aunt. She still brags that she owns the very first piece of furniture I ever made." Over the years, Patrick developed his skills, and went on to make woodwork of all types, including dressers, bedroom suites, scrollwork balusters for porches, coffee and dining tables, and chairs. "I've always wanted to learn everything there was to learn," Patrick says, "even though I know there's always something more."

Although he loves making furniture, the amount of time and effort required to market it proved an increasing drain. Along with his desire to broaden his horizons, this led Patrick to begin making smaller items such as boxes and jewelry. "Given my background, it's no surprise that my jewelry incorporates elements from my other work. I can't wait to do more one-of-a-kind pieces, though. I've got sketches and drawings for a dozen new ideas."

PYRAMID EARRINGS

- These delicate earrings begin as a laminate of nine 3/16" square rods, each 10" long, in contrasting woods such as wenge and padouk, wenge and oak, or purpleheart and maple. The boxes that house them are fabricated in the same way, except that their rod dimension is 1" square.
- For the box, prepare stock and glue a laminate block as shown in illustration **Leonard 1**. Crosscut the block to 3" lengths.
- Using the tablesaw miter fence, mill the 3" blocks into pyramid shapes.
- Bandsaw the pyramid horizontally so that **Part A**, the base, is 7/8" high, and **Part B**, the top, is 1-1/2" high.
- Using a flat-bottom drill bit, bore a 1-1/4" diameter hole 3/4" deep in **Part A**, the pyramid base.
- Sand and polish base and top.
- Mill **Part C**, a 1/8" thick square of contrasting wood to serve as the underliner for the pyramid top. (This replaces the material that was removed when the top was sliced off, thus restoring the smooth outer profile of the pyramid). Sand **Part C** and glue it to the underside of **Part B**, the top.
- Drill a 1/8" diameter hole 1/4" deep in one corner of the base and top.
- Apply two coats of water-based lacquer to the pyramid.
- When dry, install **Part D**, a 1/8" diameter attachment dowel 7/16" in length.
- To make the earrings, repeat the first three steps using 3/16" square stock.
Create the pyramid shape using a sanding disc or the flat platen of a stationary 6"x 48" belt sander.
- Drill a 1/16 diameter hole as close to the top of each earring as possible.
- Apply a water-based lacquer, then install earring wires.

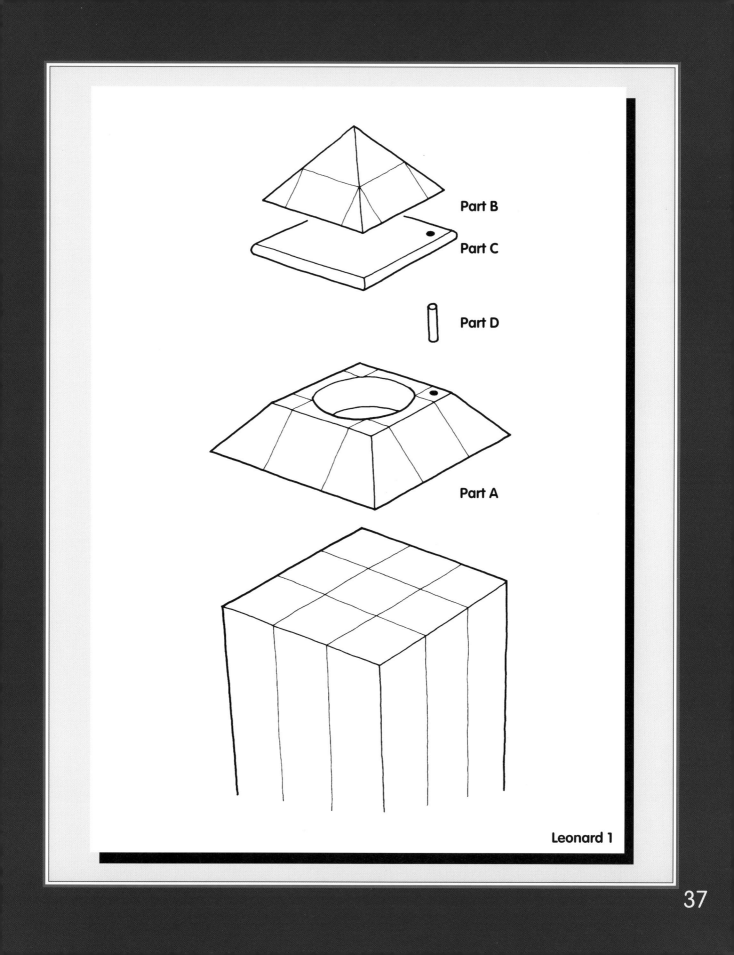

Part B

Part C

Part D

Part A

Leonard 1

Photo by Olan Mills

L O R I
G L I C K

My Dad was in the Air Force, so when I was growing up we moved around a lot. I've always loved to create, and from as far back as I can remember I wanted to become an artist. I've always had very strong beliefs about how I want things to look; maybe the fact that my external world changed so frequently contributed to that."

Lori Glick drew and painted all through elementary and high school, then studied weaving, ceramics, photography, and finally woodworking in college. "I decided that teaching art wasn't for me, so I needed a creative medium in which I could earn my own living," she recalls in her Northern California studio. "At first, I was intimidated by woodwork. This was fifteen years ago, at a time when you just didn't see women in the workshop. Everything was brand new, and it was pretty scary. I cried a lot.

"Fortunately I had great friends and great teachers: a wood-turning professor with the ability to make what he was doing really exciting, and a fellow student who suggested we start selling our work at local craft fairs. Now that I've gotten myself established, I can't imagine doing anything else.

"The kind of person I am doesn't leave me with much choice: I have to be creative. I feel so rewarded at the end of the day, knowing I've made something completely new, that wouldn't have come into being without me — particularly when it started out as some raggedy old board. With every piece I finish, I feel like part of my soul is in it."

• To make the circular leaf pendants on page 38, turn two 1-1/2" diameter discs 1/8" thick from contrasting wood such as madrone and rosewood, or imbuia and eucalyptus.
• Draw the design on the upper disc, and cut it out with a fine blade on the scroll saw.
• Use a Dremel or other flexible shaft tool to shape, roundover, and detail the design, making certain it stays connected to the outer rim of the disc in at least two places.
• Polish the surface of the blank backing disc and glue it under the design. Apply spray lacquer. Screw in two threaded rings and attach chain.

• To carve the shell and leaf brooches, start with a 2" square blank of padouk or boxwood 1/4" thick. Draw the design on the blank, and cut it out on the scroll saw.
• Use a Dremel or other flexible shaft tool to shape, roundover, and detail.
• Polish the surfaces and apply a hand-rubbed oil finish.
• Attach a pin back.

• To make the Greenhouse pendant, use the bandsaw and chisels to create the house shape in pine or other softwood.
• With a small brush, apply water-based paint.
• Screw a threaded ring to the roof peak and attach a silk cord.

• The maple bird in the "Out on a Limb" pendant is carved and finished in the same way as the circular pendants.
• Select a 3" long section of camphorwood or other natural twig. Attach bird to twig using a #4 x 1/2" screw.
• Screw two threaded rings to the twig and attach a silk cord.

• For the birdseye maple and amethyst necklace and earring set, mill three 1/8" thick pieces of maple 1" wide and 2-1/4" long.

• Draw the design on the wood and cut out using the scroll saw.

• With a Dremel or other flexible shaft tool, clean up the curved piercing cuts, carve the relief detail, smooth, and polish.

• Apply a hand-rubbed oil finish.

• Select a matched pair of amethyst or other semiprecious stones about 3/32" in diameter, and a slightly larger single stone about 1/4" in diameter. Choose a drill bit to match and mill shallow holes in the workpieces.

• Glue the stones in place. Screw in threaded rings and attach chain and earring wires.

Photo by David hill

KAREN SCATES

Karen Scates didn't like to be indoors when she was a child. "I was the oldest kid, and cooking and sewing didn't appeal to me. Fortunately, my grandfather built a little woodshop, and in between making molasses and stacking hay, we'd do woodworking together."

Karen's professional career is at a Veterinary Hospital, which has two advantages for her craft: she is able to study animals close-up, and she has access to surgical equipment catalogs, which provide tools that are useful in making her miniatures. Precision clamps, tiny tweezers and hemostats, surgical scalpels, and fine wire sutures all play a role in her Kentucky workshop.

"I've always been fascinated with miniature things. When I started out, all I had was a few hand tools, so small carvings were about all I could make. I like to feel the work, and be able to see where I'm at, so I still do all my carving and sanding by hand. I'm also a believer in close observation, and I collect a lot of books and source materials. Whether it's birds and animals in nature, or musical instruments, if I like it, I'm going to try to duplicate it in miniature."

- For animal pins such as the horse design which utilize the natural color of the wood, start with a 2-1/2" x 2-1/2" x 1/4" block of mahogany or other hardwood. Designs that will be painted, such as the butterfly or hummingbird, may be made from hardwood or close-grained softwood.
- For small-scale close-up work of this nature, use binocular magnifying glasses in magnifications ranging from 2x to 10x.
- Draw the design in pencil on the workpiece.
- Use a scroll saw to cut out the design.
- With carving knives, scalpel, or flexible shaft tool, carve, detail and smooth the piece.
- Apply acrylic paint with a fine brush. Iridescent powders may be added to the paint to produce effects like those in the hummingbird.
- When dry, apply brush-on or spray lacquer. Attach a pin back.

- Karen's instrument pins are accurate 1/12th scale reproductions, complete with strings made from surgical steel sutures, and turnable tuning pegs. They are made using the same techniques as full-size instruments.

Photo by Sears Photo Studio

SUSAN LONG

Susan Long received her Master of Fine Arts Degree in Jewelry and Metalsmithing from the Texas Women's University in 1982. She married a woodworker the next year, which gave her the opportunity to incorporate wood in her jewelry designs.

"I found wood to be a nice contrast to metal, which is so rigid," Susan says. "Wood has a softness to it, and a naturalness to its textures and colors."

Today, Susan designs the jewelry, and her husband has developed the techniques necessary to produce it. From their home and studio, located in the oldest brick building in Denton County, Texas, their work has found its way into national magazines, the Smithsonian Institute, and galleries and museum shops nationwide.

• To make the parallelogram earrings, each of which has a finished width of 3/4", start by fabricating a laminate block of ebony, padouk, and dyed veneer following the instructions on page13.
• Bandsaw 1/8" thick sections from the laminate. Draw the earring design on these sections, and cut out.
• Shape, round, and polish on the belt sander. Apply a hand-rubbed oil finish.
• Screw in threaded rings.
• Make the beads from another section of the original laminate. When oiled, place a predrilled onyx bead on a long-shank threaded ring, and attach to each bead. Connect these rings to the rings on the base of the earring. Attach an earring back.

• The beaded bracelet and necklace combine laminated wood beads with beads of tigereye, garnet, hematite, and bocote. Make the laminate beads following the procedure for earrings, above. Drill a 1/32" diameter holes through each, then apply an oil finish.
• Carve and shape the bocote and ebony necklace pendants, and screw on threaded rings.
• String the beads and attach clasp.

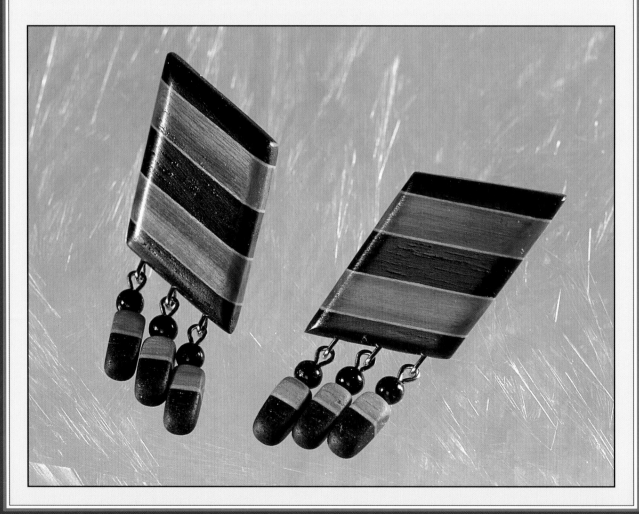

Photo by Tracie Taylor

K R I S
T A Y L O R

Currently working as the Art Director of a textile mill, Kris Taylor has been an artist, art teacher, and fabric designer all her adult life. A number of her fabric designs have been purchased by national manufacturers and put in "repeat"; that is, printed in large quantities in different colors, and sold for use in clothing and home furnishings.

"The theme of pattern runs through everything I do," Kris writes from her Pennsylvania studio. "It shows in these jewelry pieces, as well as in my painting, my textile designs, and the work I do at the textile mill."

To make her jewelry, Kris assembles beads, bangles, bits of exotic woods from a carver friend, cedar from an old cigar box, even a rubber snake. On some of the wood elements she adds her own painted designs. Each of these eclectic materials, of course, has its own pattern.

"I have an incredible collection of 'what-not's,'" Kris says. "For years I used to shop the New York City bead district, and I got to know which stores had the most amazing stuff. I also shop yard sales for odds and ends of old jewelry, which I take apart to salvage what I can use."

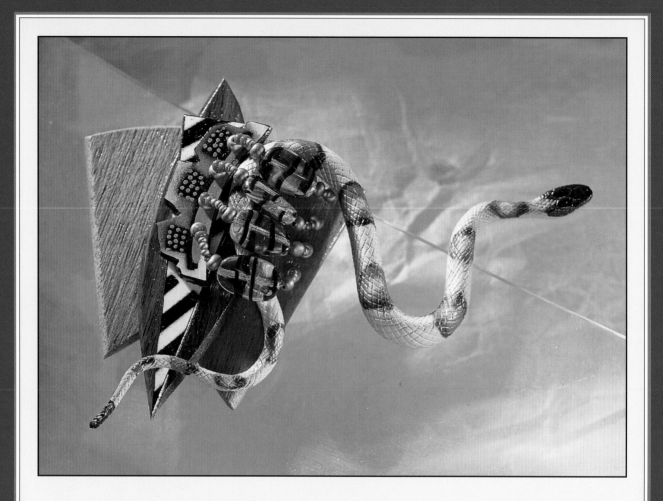

Constructed Pins

• Mill 1/8" thick pieces of 4" x 4" solid hardwood, such as ebony, wenge, cedar, or mahogany. These will be used as both backing and intermediate layers.

• Draw irregular linear and/or curved shapes, as suggested by the photographs, and cut out on the bandsaw. Sand faces and edges.

• Detail some of the intermediate and upper layers of wood using brushed and sprayed acrylic paints.

• Apply a spray lacquer to the wooden elements.

• Assemble the layers into pin forms using small quantities of adhesive.

• With a 1/32" drill bit, drill holes as needed for attachment of beads and other design elements that have attachment shafts.

• Assemble design elements into the finished piece.

• Attach a pin backing.

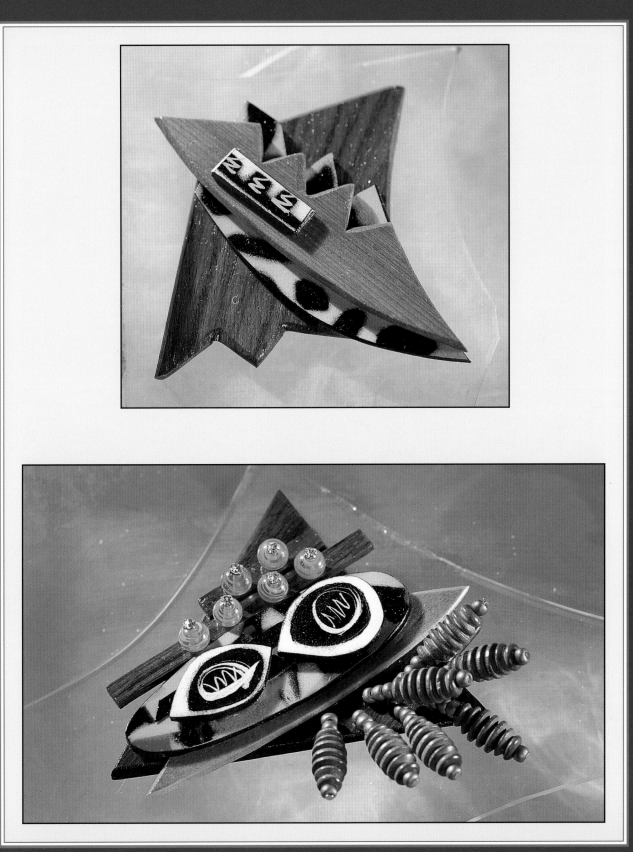

DAVID MARSON

Trained as a geologist, David Marson didn't begin working in wood until after he had graduated from college and served in the armed forces. "A carpenter friend of mine invited me to help him building a house, and that got me interested in making things. Now my inspiration can be anything from studies in geological stratigraphy to a romantic journey through the American Southwest. It all combines easily on the blackboard of my mind, and I find I can skip the sketches and get right to the finished product."

Moving to an acreage in Arkansas, David found himself doing more carpentry, along with plumbing and electrical work, and whatever else needed to be done. This left him with a good set of tools, along with easy access to walnut, cherry, hackberry, sycamore, oak, and other native Ozark hardwoods. Inspired by friends working in craft, he began making folding furniture.

Since then, assisted by his wife Kathryn, he has focussed on making jewelry. David's work is distinguished by the glowing colors of his intricate symmetrical designs, created by slicing and shifting handmade laminates. He has also developed a technique for incorporating sterling silver into his work, which has won major awards, and is featured in fine craft galleries throughout the country.

The symmetrical chevron pattern in these designs consists of hardwood solids, hardwood veneers and dyed veneers. The woods used include maple, purpleheart, tulipwood, wenge, rosewood, and cherry. One style incorporates sections of sheet silver, glued with epoxy in place of wood veneer.

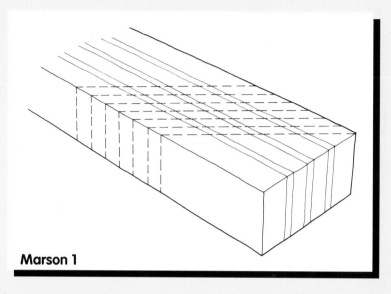

Marson 1

• As shown in illustration **Marson 1**, make a laminate block approximately 1" x 2"x 10" following the procedure outlined on page 13.
• When dry, mill sections across the laminate block at a 45-degree angle as indicated by the dotted lines in illustration **Marson 1**. The thinner the sections, the more intricate the design.

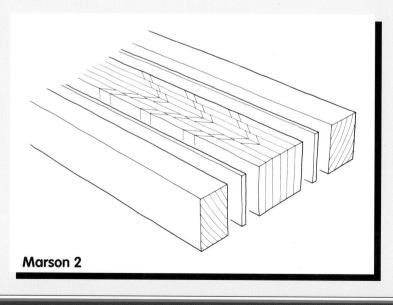

Marson 2

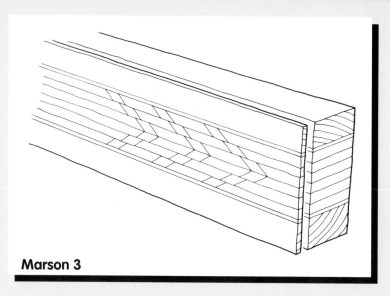

Marson 3

• Reassemble the sections into a second laminate, arranging them in mirror image or book-match pattern so that they form the chevron design. (Illustration **Marson 2**). On either side of the central chevron, add Part A, a 1/32" wide strip of contrasting wood, such as the dyed blue veneer shown in the photographs, and Part B, a 1/4" wide outer strip of solid hardwood.
• Glue the new laminate block. When dry, bandsaw into 1/32" thick sections, as shown in illustration **Marson 3**.

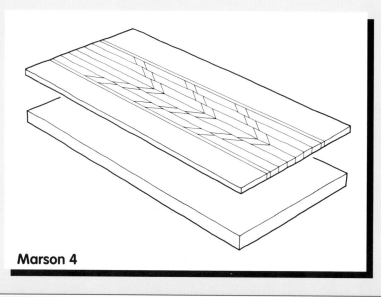

Marson 4

• Prepare a substrate of contrasting solid wood, and glue the laminate section to it (illustration **Marson 4**). The dimensions of this substrate will vary depending on the intended finish size of the workpiece.

• The completed blank may now be bandsawn to the desired earring shape (illustration **Marson 5**). Drill a 1/32" diameter hole at the one end of the earring. Shape, sand, and polish.

• Apply two coats of water-based spray lacquer, and attach earring wires.

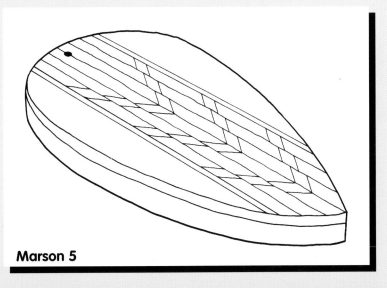

Marson 5

Photo by Stephen Petegorsky

S H I N I C H I
M I Y A Z A K I

After being educated and trained as an artist in Japan, Shinichi Miyazaki came to the United States and began to work with wood, creating sculpture and designing and building furniture. (One of his chairs is in the permanent collection of the Smithsonian Institute.) After a ten-year detour through the New York fashion world, where he designed and produced handpainted clothing, the artist settled in rural Massachusetts to refocus his attention on wood.

"The wood I prefer to work with is indigenous maple, cherry, plum, apple, or beech from the region around my studio. Usually the trees are very old, ones that time and nature have had a chance to work with. My supply comes from local farmers, woodsmen, and road crews who can't bear to turn a beautiful old tree into firewood.

"I begin with huge unmilled sections, and cut the wood in a way that will reveal the artistry lying within. Some pieces are spalted; others include decades-old maple sugar tap-holes, which can produce anything from soft, brushy watercolor-like markings to distinct, deeply colored spots."

Miya combines these local woods with ebony, rosewood, teak, black palm, and purpleheart in subtle designs that appear quite simple. "I love the simplicity," he says. "But it takes a great deal of work to make it look easy."

63

HAIRCOMBS

• The ebony and teak combs begin as 1/4" thick pieces of hardwood 2" x 3-1/2", and 3-1/2" x 3-3/4", respectively.
• Create the teeth of the comb by using the bandsaw to mill parallel slots, each the width of the sawblade. These are milled in a semicircular pattern for the ebony comb, and a parabolic pattern for the teak comb.
• Shape and sand on the 6" x 48" belt sander.
• Smooth the edges of the bandsaw cuts by hand with a fine-tooth file.
• Apply a hand-rubbed oil finish.
• To make the ebony and purpleheart comb, mill a piece of ebony 1/4" x 1-3/4" x 1-3/4", and a piece of purpleheart 1/4" x 1-1/2" x 3-1/2".
• Overlap the pieces and bandsaw at a 15-degree angle to produce the two parts shown in the photograph.
• Glue the two parts together.

- Shape the outline of the comb on the belt sander.
- With the bandsaw, cut out three 1/8" wide slots. (Note that the slots are wide because this style of comb is designed to be inserted in a hairstyle as an accent.)
- With files and hand sanding, round over and polish all surfaces.
- Apply a hand-rubbed oil finish.
- Follow the same procedure to make the 7-1/2" long two-pronged ebony comb with the circular spalted maple tip.

BROOCHES AND BARRETTES

• To make the brooches and barrettes, mill 1/4" thick pieces of spalted or other interesting-looking wood in square or rectangular shapes of any size between 1" and 5".
• Using the flat platen and the idler pulley of the 6" x 48" belt sander as cutting surfaces, shape the pieces with a 150 grit belt into symmetrical or irregular shapes as shown in the photograph.
• Apply a spray lacquer, and glue on pin or barrette backs.

BRACELETS

• Bracelets begin as 1/2" x 5" x 5" pieces of maple, ebony, zebrawood, rosewood, or other figured wood.
• Attach a 3" diameter hole saw to the drill press and remove the center of each piece of wood. (Vary the diameter of the hole saw to create bracelets that will fit wrists of varying sizes).
• With a file and hand sanding, round and smooth the hole saw cut.
• Bandsaw the exterior circumference of the bracelet. This cut may be made either as a circle, or as a slight oblong shape, as shown in the photographs.
• Use the 6" x 48" belt sander to shape and contour the bracelet as desired.
• Apply a hand-rubbed oil finish to the finished bracelet.

INRO PURSES

These wooden containers or Inro, designed to hang around the neck on a silk cord, were traditionally used by travellers to carry potions to protect them on long journeys. Reinterpreted today as jewelry, the shapes retain their talismanic power.

In the smaller versions, the lid is held in place atop the body by cords running through holes, along which it slides open. These holes extend into the body of the container, where they are anchored with glue.

- Start with a block of figured or spalted hardwood slightly larger than the finished sizes of the styles shown, which are 3/4" x 2-1/4" x 2-1/2"; 7/8" x 3-1/2" x 4-1/4"; and 2" x 4" x 7-1/2".
- With a 1/8" diameter drill bit, drill a hole 1/4" in from the outer edge of both sides of the block. The depth of this hole, into which the cord will be glued, is determined by the final dimensions of the piece.
- Shape the container on the belt sander.
- Bandsaw off the lid.
- Use a router with a carbide bit to rout out the interior space.
- Sand and polish. Apply a hand-rubbed oil finish. When dry, attach the cord.

BUZZ COREN

As a young man, Buzz Coren's ambition was to become a scientist. Like so many wood-workers, however, during college his interests changed, and although he still keeps bees near his North Carolina workshop, he decided not to pursue a career in biology.

Inspired by the example of a friend who started a craft business, Buzz began experimenting with jewelry and small boxes. "Everybody wanted to buy what I made," Buzz recalls. "My work sold really well at the first craft show I got into. It was like getting a paycheck, so I quit my job the next day.

"I learned the basics of woodworking from my father, who was always working on projects around the house. He'd do things like let me hold the end of the board while he sawed, so when I started taking woodshop in high school, I wasn't afraid of tools."

Although largely self-taught, Buzz has become a master of the technique of lamination. He writes, "Small changes in laminating, stacking, or angle setting result in major differences in the look of the finished piece. Combined with the wide spectrum of wood and veneer available, this allows limitless possibilities in form and pattern. I feel blessed with the ability to work and play with this wonderful resource of wood. I stay amazed at its versatility, precious importance, and inherent beauty."

• To make the brooches and earrings, use dyed veneers to fabricate laminate blocks following the instructions on page 13. Bandsaw these laminate blocks into 1/8" thick sections in varying widths and at varying angles. 90-degree, 45-degree, and irregular angles will produce differing effects. For the pinwheel brooch shown in the photograph, bandsaw the laminate into wedges, each tapering from 1/4" wide to as narrow as possible. The lengths of the wedges vary from 1-1/8" to 1-3/8".

• Reassemble the sections to produce the final design.

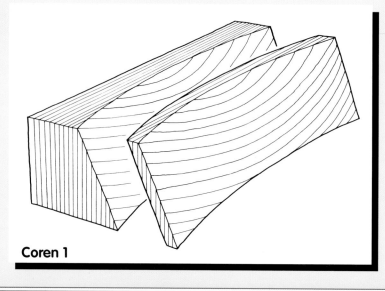

Coren 1

• The curved pattern of the large barrette is made by slicing the laminate block at an angle off the vertical, as shown in Illustration **Coren 1**. When sanded, the laminates will form the curved shape.

• Apply a spray finish, and attach appropriate backing.

Photo by Tom Raffelt

T . B R E E Z E
V E R D A N T

Although he has long been a master of conventional marquetry, with its floral motifs and repeated geometric designs, T. Breeze VerDant's latest work takes the technique into new territories of abstraction. Some of the geometric elements remain, but the fluid shapes and fascinating color combinations he is currently producing in his Vermont studio now suggest imaginary, almost psychological landscapes.

"I have a long history with trees," Breeze remembers. "As a child, I could always be found up in them. As an adult, I logged them to build myself a log cabin, and to produce enough firewood to see me through the long Adirondack winters. I never cease to be awed by trees, by their inward and outward beauty, and respectful of the essential role they play in all aspects of our life.

"I like the fact that while my work celebrates trees, it has a minimal impact on them. I use native hardwoods, as well as scrap and cutoffs whenever I can. Marquetry is an ancient craft, one that combines the natural and the artistic in a way I like. With it, I feel I've found a chance to achieve my goal: to stun people with the beauty of wood grain, and be happy doing it."

• To make these marquetry pins, start by assembling veneers of natural hardwoods, including domestic species such as sycamore, boxwood, hickory, walnut, maple, koa, hop hornbeam, lacewood, and holly, along with imported species such as rosewood, tulipwood, ebony, wenge, and narra. These may be purchased from veneer suppliers, or handmade in the shop by slicing thin sections off a larger block using the bandsaw.

• Stack two layers of veneer, and draw the design outline on the top layer.

• Using a surgical scalpel or other sharp, fine-pointed cutting tool, cut the outline through both layers at once. Trim and fit the veneer pieces as needed.

• Prepare several additional pieces of veneer in contrasting woods, each slightly larger than the intended size of the finished piece. These will be laminated into a backing or substrate for the marquetry.

• Using the technique for laminates described on page 13, glue the design and any number of substrate layers into a single laminate block approximately 1/4" thick.

• Trim the resulting block and bandsaw to desired shape.
• Use a 6" x 48" belt sander to smooth the top marquetry surface, being careful not to sand through the design.
• Shape the edges of the design on the flat platen or curved idler cylinder of the sander. Note in the photographs how the vertical edges of each pin are bevelled to show the contrasting wood layers of the substrate.
• Apply a spray lacquer finish, and attach a pin back.

STAG BEETLE

Photo by Brian Blauser

MINDY & LARRY KING

I announced to my eighth grade shop teacher that I wanted to be a woodworker," recalls Mindy King. "I guess I was an early bloomer when it came to women choosing a career in a traditionally male field. Fortunately for me, my teacher was very supportive."

After high school, Mindy studied furniture design at the Rochester Institute of Technology, and began her professional career building musical instruments. Along the way, she married Larry King, a biology teacher with an interest in science and math who also liked to build sculptures. One of his pieces was a large wire Cartesian graph that he had covered, somewhat tongue-in-cheek, with handmade spiders.

To Larry's surprise, everybody wanted to buy the spiders. This inspired Mindy to make spider earrings, which became so successful that the couple found themselves in a new business. Because it was so much more fun than what they had been doing, they dubbed their new enterprise "Mirthworks."

Mindy's skill as a professional woodworker matched perfectly with Larry's knowledge of insects. "From the start, our designs were biologically driven," Larry recalls. "We'd choose an insect, and then Mindy would figure out what woodworking techniques we could use to reproduce it.

"We sell a lot of the appealing insects, like ladybugs and dragonflies, but we also make some of the less popular ones, like wasps, mosquitoes and ticks. It's fun to listen to people's reactions. Young people and old people are the ones who most want to wear our insect jewelry. The young haven't yet lost their fascination with the marvels of the natural world. The old have fond memories of their youth, including insects, and besides, they no longer care what anybody else thinks about what they wear."

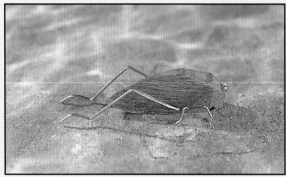

KATYDID

GRASSHOPPER

• To make the angular-bodied insects (Katydid, Grasshopper), start with 1/2" square blocks, 2-1/4" long, of any available light-colored hardwood. The Katydid was made from a laminate; to fabricate, follow the procedures on page 13.
• Use the stationary belt sander with a 150 grit belt to mill the angular, faceted shape of the insect body. Sand lightly by hand with 220 grit sandpaper to smooth sharp edges.
• Wearing protective gloves and clothing, and following manufacturer's instructions, dye the solid hardwood bodies as desired with water-based dye.
• Drill 1/32" diameter attachment holes for the wires that will form the antennae and legs. (Insects have six legs, which distinguishes them from Arthropods, such as Crabs and Spiders, which have eight.)
• Apply a spray coat of shellac. (As Mindy King notes, shellac is especially appropriate because it's a bug product to begin with — the main ingredient in genuine shellac is produced by insects.)

BUMBLE BEE

PAPER WASP

DOODLEBUG

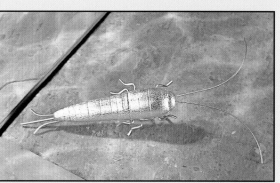
SILVERFISH

• Cut sections of 1/32" diameter brass wire for the antennae and legs.
• For larger insects such as the Grasshopper, use a hammer to flatten the first joint of the rear leg. With needlenose pliers, bend wires to appropriate shape and insert.
• Attach a stud or pin back.

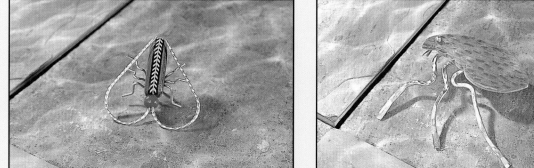
LONGHORN BEETLE
FLEA

• The bodies of the insects with a symmetrical radial axis are turned on a Klein lathe, specially designed for small-scale projects such as these by Bonnie Klein, whose work is featured on page 130. The Honeybee and Paper Wasp are made of stained ash; the Stag Beetle is a laminate; the Doodlebug is a stained store-bought birch screw-hole plug; the Silverfish is maple covered with silver leaf; and the Longhorn Beetle is a section of guitar-purfling, detailed with red paint. The body of the Flea is shaped on the sander from lacewood veneer.
• After the insect form has been turned, polished, stained, and coated with shellac, drill holes for the wings, antennae, and legs as needed.
• Fabricate these appendages from brass wire, creating the flattened profiles and twisted, curved, or angled shapes as desired using hammer and needlenose pliers.
• Attach stud or pin back.

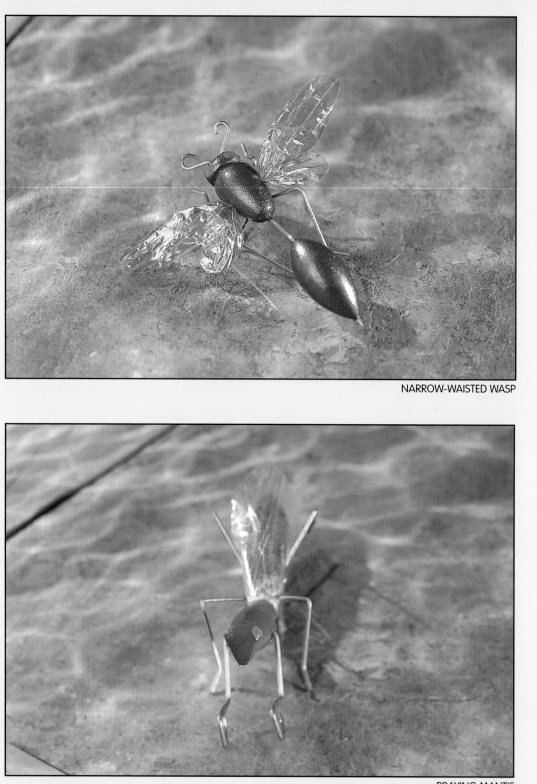

NARROW-WAISTED WASP

PRAYING MANTIS

CICADA

DRAGONFLY

• The Narrow-Waisted Wasp, Praying Mantis, Cicada, and Dragonfly are fabricated on the lathe and sander following the procedures described above. Apply colors using a nontoxic spray paint.
• Drill holes for the brass legs and antennae as needed. Drill 3/32" holes for the wings.
• Install the antennae and legs.
• To make the wings, cut out sections of colored sheet Mylar or similar plastic. Twist the ends and glue into the wing holes.
• Attach stud or pin back.

LEAFHOPPER

83

Photo by Bob Barrett

JUDY DITMER

I knew I was an artist when I was four years old, but it took me a long time to find my medium," Judy Ditmer writes from her Ohio studio. As one of the country's leading woodturners, as well as the author of books on turning bowls and wooden jewelry, Judy's persistence has clearly paid off.

"As a child, I always liked to make things, and to take things apart and figure out how they work. I never got much encouragement, though, even when I went to art school, and I'd about given up on being able to do art for a living when I discovered woodturning. I happened to go to a conference on turning, and got just blown out of the water. 'This is it,' I thought to myself, 'this is what I've been looking for.'

"What I like about turning is that the design process and the making process are so integrated. You don't start with a paper-and-pencil drawing, then set out to build it. Instead, you're making decisions as you do the cutting. It's a subtractive process: the result you're after is right there in the wood, waiting. When you reach that pre-existing final form, there's such a sense of rightness."

Judy's jewelry is made from a wide variety of domestic and imported hardwoods, and incorporates accents of colored inks, metals, ceramics, plastics, and semiprecious stones such as yellow jade. The woods used include bocote, African boxwood, leadwood, greenheart, lignum, dogwood, fishtail oak, maple, American hornbeam, pink ivory, and ebony.

• The earrings and pins are made by combining sections of bowl-shaped turnings that are cut on the endgrain of hardwood spindles. As detailed in Judy Ditmer's book, "Turning Wooden Jewelry" (Published by Schiffer), prepare 2" diameter stock of any convenient length in a variety of hardwoods. Attach to the lathe, and turn shallow bowl shapes in thicknesses varying from 1/8" to 1/4.
• Use the bandsaw to cut the completed shapes into semicircles, quarter circles, and other shapes as desired.

• Make a rough assembly of shapes for a particular pin or pair of earrings. As needed, detail the shapes with contrasting colors using an ink pen, or acrylic paint applied with a small brush.
• Glue the sections together to form the final shape.
• If needed, drill a 1/32" diameter hole for attaching earring wire.
• Apply spray lacquer. When dry, attach appropriate backing.

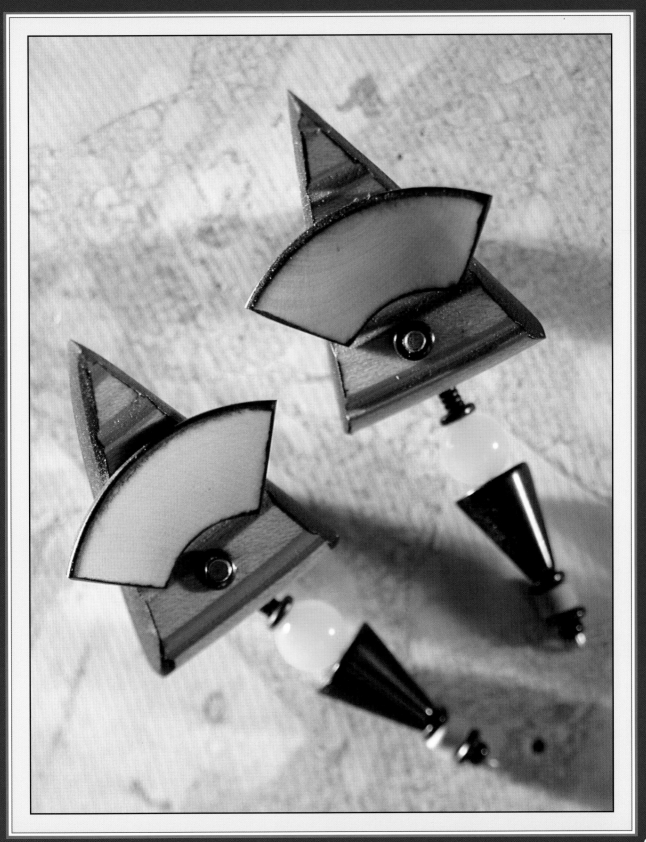

WILLIAM
CHAPPELOW

William Chappelow was pursuing a degree in oceanography when he decided to try out a more pioneer-type life-style. "As a career, oceanography didn't feel quite right," he remembers, "and I found myself headed into the mountains."

During a winter storm, a massive oak fell in the woods where William was living by Cuyamaca Lake, in the Southern California hill country. A few days later, he used a branch from that tree to stir the cauldron in which he was making natural soap. Sitting by the fire that evening, he found himself carving and embellishing the crude piece of oak into his first stirring tool, and as time passed, that tree proved a wellspring of spoons, "spurtles" and other kitchen implements.

Over the next few years, William and a partner founded a woodworking business, which they named Tryyn (pronounced "treen") after the old English term for a style of functional woodwork, and opened a studio near San Diego. Since then, William's carvings, kitchenware, and jewelry have been exhibited in some of the finest galleries in the country, and he has been honored by seeing his work purchased for the private collections of British Royalty and United States Presidents.

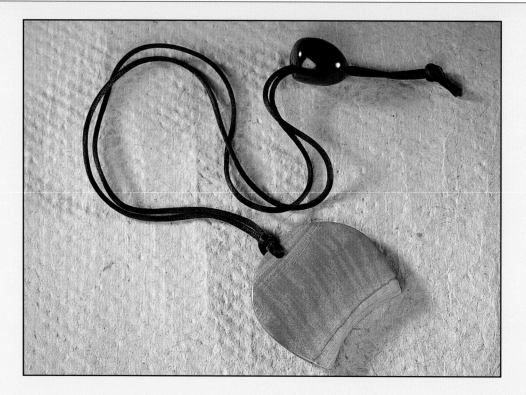

CARVED PENDANTS

These carved and polished pendants are made of osage orange (yellow, 3" long); coral tree (round, 2-1/4" diameter); pink ivory wood (2-3/4" wide); cocobolo (sharp-pointed arrowhead, 2-1/8" long); and California manzanita (3-1/4" long).

• Select a piece of highly figured, brightly colored, or interestingly flawed hardwood. Using a bandsaw, mill the workpiece into a rough pendant shape in such a way as to preserve and highlight the figure, color, or flaw.

• With carving tools, belt sander, or drum sander, finalize the rough shape. Be certain to save irregularities and defects, such as the void in the round "coin pendant" (see photo page 88), or the sapwood in the pink ivory and the arrowhead (page 93). These give each piece its distinctive personality.

• Follow the same procedure to make beads, such as the ebony bead on the pink ivory wood pendant. Beads may also be made from bone, or store-bought ceramic, glass, or metal.

• Using the drill press, drill a 1/8" diameter hole as close as is practical to the top edge of the pendant.

• Round the edges, smooth the faces, and polish all surfaces, either by hand, or with belt or drum sander.

• Apply a hand-rubbed oil finish. When dry, rub with fine steel wool, wax, and buff.

• Using an electric engraving pencil with a fine tip, sign each piece.

• String pendant, along with a bead if desired, on a silk cord.

WALRUS NECKLACE

• Mill two 6" lengths of purpleheart or similar brightly-colored wood, each 3-1/2" wide and 1" thick, and a 2" cube of ebony. For the beads, mill two 3/8" ebony cubes.
• With a pencil, draw the tusk shapes on the purpleheart. Rough-cut using the bandsaw. Bandsaw the corners off the large ebony cube.
• Drill a 1/8" diameter hole in the thick ends of each tusk, and through the centers of the ebony cubes.
• Sand the workpieces on the drum sander to perfect the shapes. Change to progressively finer grits to polish.
• Apply a hand-rubbed oil finish. When dry, rub with fine steel wool, wax, and buff.
• Using an electric engraving pencil with a fine tip, sign each piece.
• String the necklace, along with a bead if desired, on a silk cord.

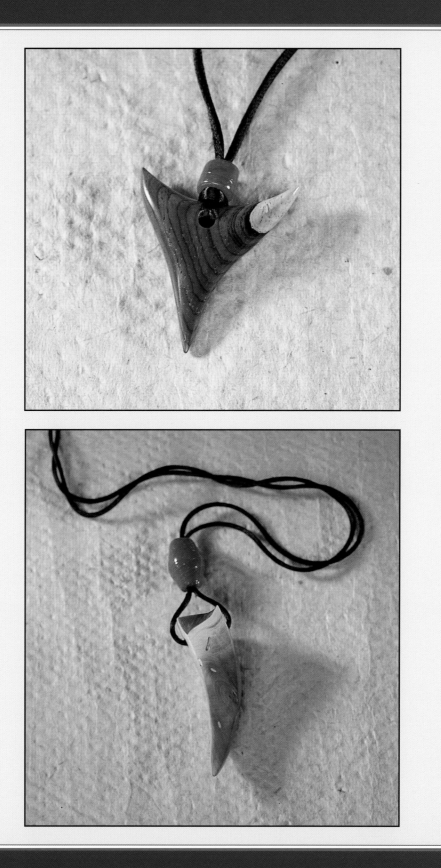

Photo by Curtis Almquist

TOM ALLEN

During his college years, Tom Allen's focus was on graphic design, a field in which he planned to make his career after graduation. One of his professors was a woodcarver, however, and it was not too long before Tom bought himself a set of chisels. "It was Easter at the time," Tom recalls, "and the first thing I carved was a three-foot tall Easter Island head."

For the next ten years, Tom's profession was graphic design, but he kept at woodworking as a hobby, gradually acquiring more tools, and eventually a studio. Like so many woodworkers, he had been giving his work to friends and family for years when someone finally said, "You ought to be selling this!" The advice took, and Tom moved to the Oregon mountains and started his woodworking business, which he calls "The Joy of Doing."

Combining familiar, abstract, and sensual shapes, Tom uses carving, inlay, bone, silver, and semiprecious stones in his jewelry, which is inspired by the natural world around him. "I like using different materials in my pieces. The carving itself has a certain effect, which is enhanced by the presence of other visual elements. In this respect, my graphic design background has been useful. Currently I'm working on larger, two-dimensional landscape-based wall pieces, but I still include fine details in turquoise, abalone, azurite, and lapis."

MIXED-MEDIA PINS

The pins and earrings shown in the photographs range from natural forms, such as the sea otter, heart, and double shell, to pure abstractions. The materials used are ebony, bocote, rosewood, padouk, boxwood, bone, abalone shell, cocobolo, bubinga, turquoise, silver wire, and silver tubing.

• Begin by sketching a design, either a natural or abstract shape. Refine the sketch and simplify it to make it practical to fabricate. In the sea otter pin, for example, note how the arms and legs become extensions of the body, the mouth is eliminated, and the number of claws is reduced to a manageable two.
• For designs from nature, select pieces of wood that will accommodate the eventual shape.
• For abstract designs, select woods that have dramatic color, figure, or grain patterns.
• Draw the outline of the shape in pencil on the workpiece, and use the bandsaw to cut it out.
• Rough shape the workpiece with carving tools or on the sander.
• Drill holes of appropriate diameter for insertion of silver wire or tubing (1/16", 3/32", 1/8"), semiprecious stones (lapis, turquoise, azurite), mother-of-pearl, and abalone shell.
• Apply clear epoxy to the holes, and insert the silver wire, stones etc.
• Sand the workpieces on the drum sander to perfect the shapes. Change to progressively finer grits to polish.
• Apply a hand-rubbed oil finish. When dry, rub with fine steel wool, wax, and buff.
• Using an electric engraving pencil with a fine tip, sign each piece.
• Apply a pin back.

Photo by Jon Hirtz

SHARON WHITMORE

I have an innate sense of artistic balance and composition," writes Sharon Whitmore from her Northern California studio, "which I've refined during my years of studying. It's become almost a natural rhythm for me: I know when something looks right, and when it looks wrong, although I can't always explain why."

After earning a Bachelor of Fine Arts Degree, Sharon concentrated on developing her painting, drawing and printmaking. She soon found, however, that woodworking was a more enjoyable way to use her skills. "During college, my husband worked part-time as a carpenter and furniture maker. As a result, he had all the power tools, and we were always surrounded with scraps of beautiful wood.

" I began playing with them, and voila! Working with wood energized me, and it also had a freeing effect on my artistic creativity: the only requirement was that the wood and the jewelry I made from it had to be beautiful."

Sharon Whitmore makes her pins, earrings, pendants, and bolo ties in a wide variety of colors and shapes, using the natural colors of purpleheart, ebony, maple, padouk, rosewood, cocobolo, pink ivorywood, bubinga, and mahogany. She does not use oil or varnish in finishing her pieces. Instead, each is waxed with jeweler's rouge, then buffed to a high sheen.

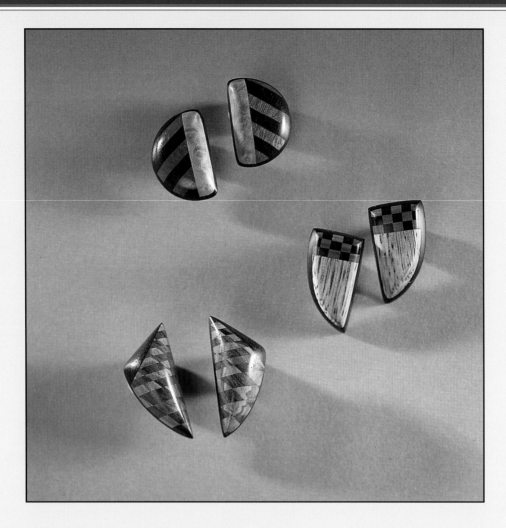

• The earrings shown in the photographs range in length from 1-1/8" to 1-7/8"; the pins range from 1-3/4" to 2-3/4". All combine sections of laminates with areas of solid wood, often mounted on a contrasting wood backing. To make them, start by producing laminate blocks in contrasting woods, following the instructions on page 13.

• Bandsaw the resulting laminate blocks into sections, and recombine these sections into new laminate blocks, using the approach shown in the projects on page 23 and page 58-61. These new combinations should be designed to produce both symmetrical and irregular patterns.

• Select portions of the laminate blocks to incorporate with solid wood in the final design, and bandsaw to desired shape.

• Prepare the solid wood portion of the design.

• Mill a 1/32" thick piece of ebony, wenge, or other dark wood to serve as the substrate for the jewelry.

• Glue laminate and solid portions to the substrate.

• Shape, sand, and polish. Apply wax and buff. Attach earring or pin backs.

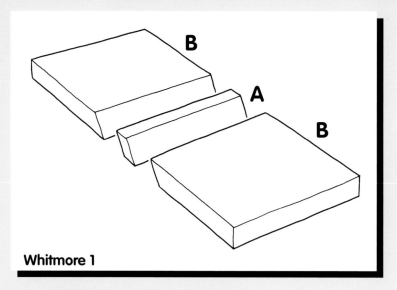

Whitmore 1

• To make pendants, follow the procedures for earrings and pins, but use stock that is 1/4" to 1/2" thick. Prior to finsh polishing, drill 1/8" diameter holes for the cords.

• Illustrations **Whitmore 1, Whitmore 2**, and **Whitmore 3** show the technique used to make the bolo tie, which features what appears to be a curved band of purpleheart. Start with a block of rosewood or other highly figured wood 1/2" x 1-1/2 "x 2-1/2". Using an angled cut, crosscut it into two pieces (Part B in **Whitmore 1**).

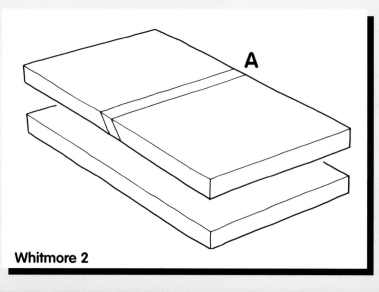

Whitmore 2

• Insert Part A, a 1/8" wide band of purpleheart or contrasting wood, and glue the assembly.
• As shown in **Whitmore 2**, glue the resulting assembly to a substrate of purpleheart.
• Draw the final shape in pencil and cut out on the bandsaw. The result will appear as illustration **Whitmore 3**. Because of the angle of the purpleheart accent stripe, when the workpiece is given its domed exterior shape, the stripe will appear to be curved.

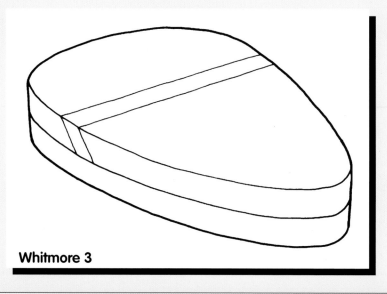

Whitmore 3

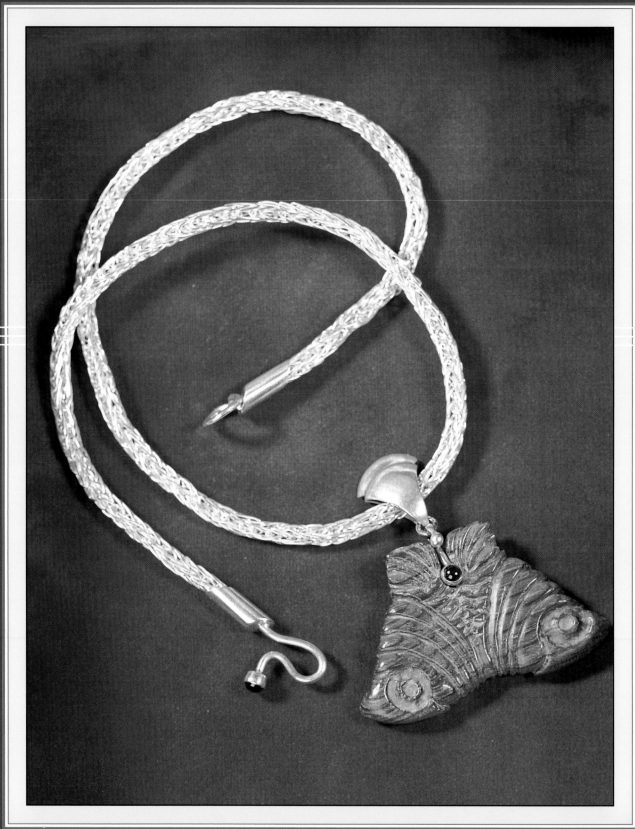

Photo by Nick Zungoli

JULIE HAMMET-CONE

Julie Hammet-Cone traces her interest in jewelry back to her early childhood. "My grandmother had a collection of jewelry, and as a little girl I remember being fascinated by her jewelry box. Everything inside it seemed magical to me: so small, so beautiful, and so personal."

Although she took courses in jewelry making throughout her schooling, Julie had always intended to become a potter. Then one day a teacher of hers said, "What do you want to be a potter for – you should be a jeweler!" The advice stuck.

Today, working in rural New York state, her inspirations are nature and music. She carves lapidary-style, as if the wood she uses were soft stone, and her mastery of jewelrymaking technique allows her to combine wood with metal in a perfect marriage.

"Wood isn't as flashy as gemstones, and it sometimes gets a limited response. But it also sets me free, because I can do anything I want with it as a material. I can move it as it moves me."

EARRINGS

The wood in the larger heart-shaped pair is rosewood, accented with a semiprecious stone called carnelian; the smaller pair is wenge, accented with fresh water pearl. The metal portions of the leaf and petal earrings are white gold.

• Using metal jewelry techniques, prepare the sterling silver setting.
• For each pair, select two 1/8" x 1" x 1" matched pieces of rosewood, wenge or other rich-looking hardwood with a pronounced grain.
• Lay the setting on the wood, draw its outline, and bandsaw.
• Carefully shape the edges of the wood insert until it makes a perfect fit with the metal form.
• Fine sand the wood, gradually proceeding up to 400 grit, and round its edges slightly.
• Glue the wood to the setting with epoxy.
• To finish, buff with a buffing compound such as white diamond or jeweler's rouge.

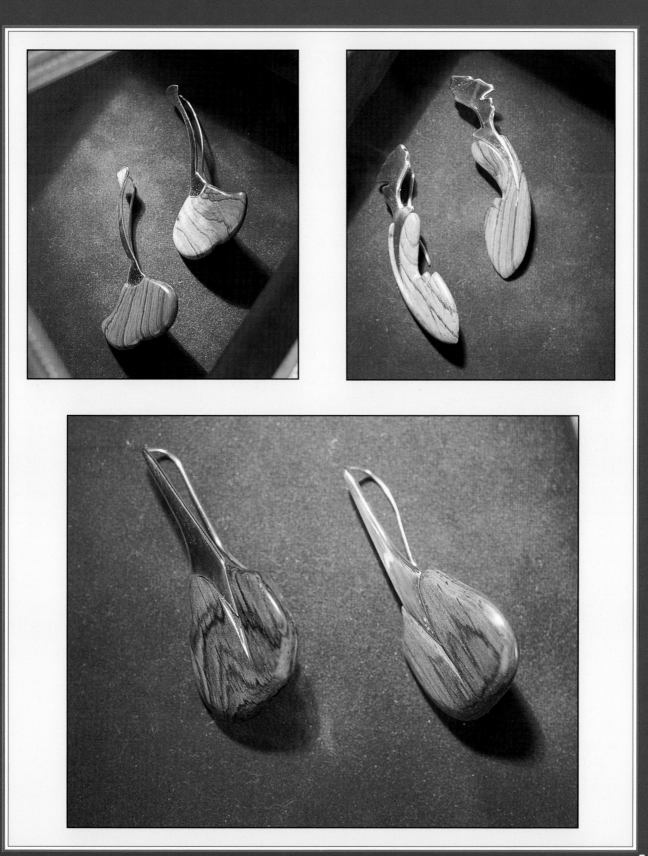

BROOCH

• Using metal jewelry techniques, prepare a sterling silver setting. Select a piece of ebony 3/8" x 3/8" x 1", and a piece of bubinga 1/4" x 1-1/2" x 2".

• Lay the setting on the wood, draw the outline, and bandsaw.

• Using sanders, carving knives, or a flexible shaft tool, shape and contour the wood. Fine sand up to 400 grit.

• Insert the teardrop-shaped ebony piece into its setting, and form the bezel or metal edge to make a snug fit. Follow the same procedure for the larger bubinga shape. Note that the bezel is carefully hammered over into the contours of the wood.

• Glue the wood to the setting with epoxy.

• To finish, buff with a buffing compound such as white diamond or jeweler's rouge.

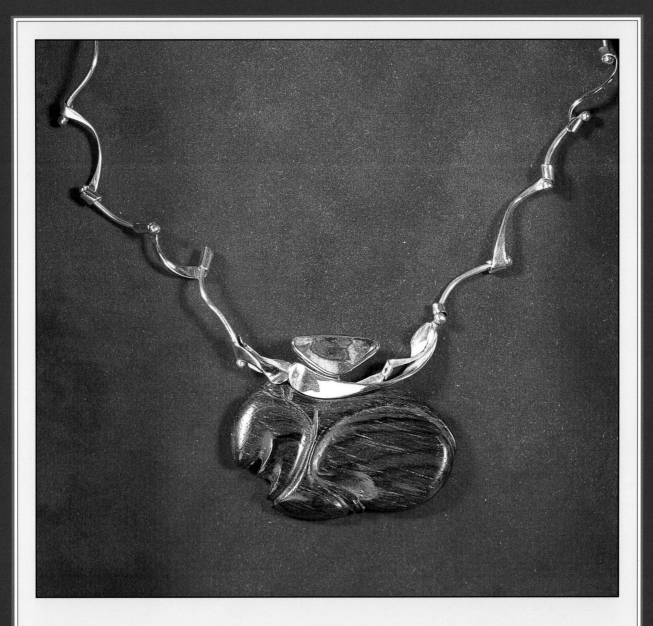

NECKLACE

The pendant in this necklace is ebony, enhanced by an Australian boulder opal. Julie Hammet-Cone hand made the silver and gold chain.

The necklace shown on page 106 is carved rosewood, accented by two garnets. Julie hand-wove the sterling silver rope from which the pendant hangs.

Photo by Tracey Baczkiewicz

P A M
M A T H E N Y

Ever since I can remember," writes Pam Matheny, "I could express myself better through art than verbally. As a child, anything I wished for I would draw. Although I studied painting and printmaking in college, I'd always had the urge work in three dimensions. When I settled in New Mexico in the 1970's, I turned to carving in stone, bone, woods, and fossil ivories.

"I sometimes felt powerless when I was young, and this led me to admire the innate strength of wild things, so animals have always been important for me. Today I live very close to nature, and the kinship I feel with wild creatures makes their images appear often in my work.

"I started out working in stone as well as in wood, but I found that I just couldn't get the freedom of form I wanted. I used to fear that wood wouldn't be valued like stone, wouldn't be held precious. But I can do what I want in wood, and the colors are so wearable, so I'm using it more and more.

"I make fetish jewelry, jewelry that has special personal meaning for the wearer. I suspect that people miss their tribalness, that tactile connection to nature, to one's personal ancientness from an infinite line of ancestors. There's no hurry — worry in life when you have your special thing with you, your mystery, and that's what my work is about."

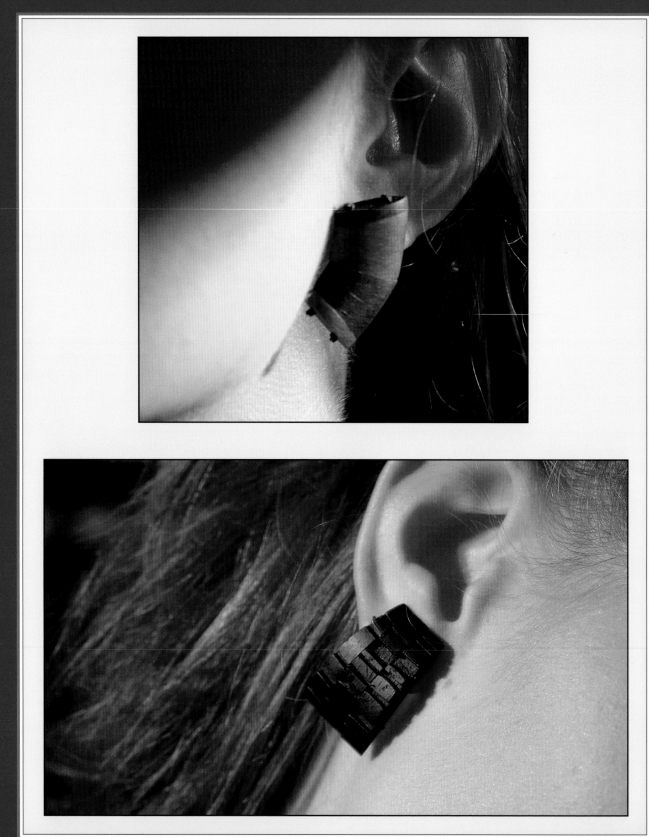

Pam Matheny's earrings and necklaces use ebony, bloodwood, rosewood, and padouk in combination with bone, jasper, and onyx. She describes her technique as follows.

• My materials come to me in rough form. Depending on whether I am dealing with wood or stone, I slab them with a band or diamond saw; from there I shape at a sanding drum or diamond wheel. Most of my carving is done with a flexible shaft tool, using steel cutters, carbide burrs, abrasive, and diamond points.

• My finishes come from hand sanding, steel wool, or polishing with sanding belts and/or oxides with dry or slurry mix on leather belts or felt buff. The wood is given a hand-rubbed oil finish.

• I hand make all my beads in much the same way. I use an ultrasonic drill to drill holes in stone pieces that are strung on wire, then turned against an abrasive wheel.

Photo by Martha Collins

MARTHA COLLINS

Making things must be in my genes," writes Martha Collins from her studio in the Olympic Mountains of Washington State. "I get such satisfaction, and such a sense ofcompletion from working with my hands. There's never been any doubt about what I wanted to do."

Martha's specialty is combining different species of hardwood with dyed veneers in intricate patterns that accentuate and complement the natural color and texture of the woods. The helical mosaic bracelets shown here, which she has been designing and making for over ten years, have been featured in several national woodworking magazines.

"I try to make sure that every piece I create makes a statement. To decide what wood patterns and combinations to use, I just follow my intuition. You put the pieces together and look at them, and if that's what works, you go with it. There are so many possibilities — that's the wonderful thing about woodworking."

In these bracelets, the technique of combining resawn laminates is expanded into three dimensions. The materials used are dyed and solid veneers, as well as rosewood, ebony, and ziricote.

• Prepare a laminate block of contrasting woods, as shown in illustration **Collins 1**. The finished block should be 2-3/4" square; its thickness may vary from 1/2" to 1-1/4". The two outside

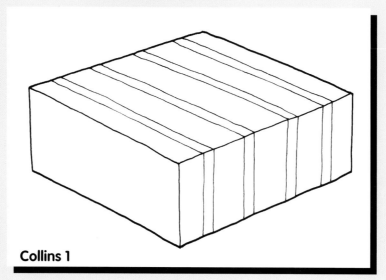

Collins 1

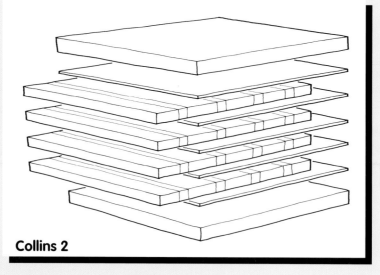

Collins 2

layers, which will form the outer edges of the bracelet, should be solid hardwood, 1/4" wide.

• Bandsaw the laminate block into sections, whose thickness may vary from 1/32" to 1/4" thick, depending on the design. Reassemble these sections into a new laminate, interspersed with 1/32" thick sheets of contrasting wood veneer, and glue (illustration **Collins 2**).

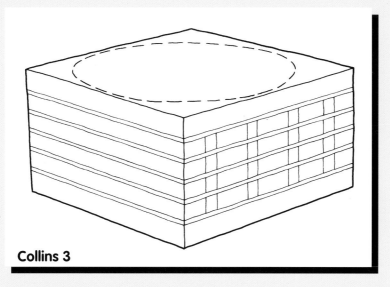

Collins 3

• Using a lathe, turn the workpiece shown in illustration **Collins 3** into a finished bracelet. The interior diameter should be 2-1/2" to 2-5/8".

• Polish and apply a hand-rubbed oil finish. Wax and buff.

TERRY EVANS

Growing up on a Kansas farm, Terry Evans has an early memory of a hand-carved stone watering trough, created by a family member in the early part of the century.

"The care and concern that went into making that trough became part of my heritage," Terry explains. "As I got older, I noticed the same qualities in other objects. I was especially impressed by the fine harness work I saw on the farm, and that got me interested in making things out of leather."

By the time he was in college, Terry had developed into an enthusiastic leather-smith. "My leather work provided me with pocket change all during college. Not long afterward, it paid the hospital bill when Mauna and I had our first child."

It was not until Terry began making inlaid wooden buckles for his leather belts that his interest shifted to wood. "I'd always loved beautiful and exotic wood, and I would meet collectors who had examples of thousands of different species. Most of the time, though, I could only get hold of small pieces, and that's why I've tended to work on a small scale ever since. My inspiration comes from two sources that don't at first seem to have much in common: the great nonobjective painter Wassily Kandinsky, and the flint hills of my native Kansas."

While evolving his unique style of inlay, Terry has continued to serve as full-time art teacher in the Kansas public schools. Although he has taught many subjects in the art curriculum, he currently teaches photography, and the photo of him above was taken by one of his students.

The technique for creating Terry Evans's intricate designs begins with laminate blocks, as described on page 13. These blocks are resawn, and the resulting sections are then glued back together in patterns that may be symmetrical or irregular, as shown in the drawings on pages 58-61.

Terry uses a variety of solid hardwoods, hardwood veneers, and dyed veneers, all of which are available by mail-order from woodworking specialty catalogs.

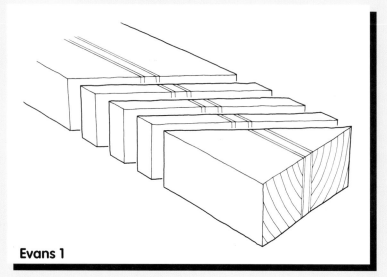

Evans 1

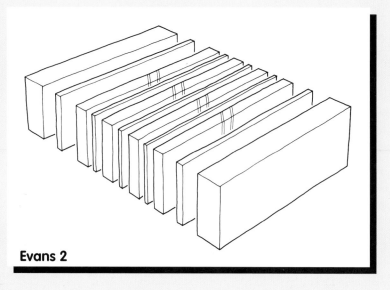

Evans 2

• To make the earrings, follow the procedures for creating and recombining laminates on pages 13, 19-23, and 58-61. Note that the beauty of these designs is enhanced by three elements: striking color combinations; the contrast between symmetrical and non-symmetrical patterns; and the large number of individual pieces of wood.

• The intricate symmetrical pattern of the pendants and bolo ties begins with a standard laminate block. As shown in illustration **Evans 1**, mill this block at an angle into 1/4" wide sections.

• Interspersing the laminate sections with solid bands of varying widths and colors, re-glue to form a second laminate block (see illustration **Evans 2**).

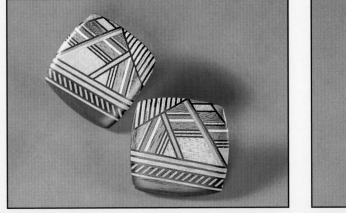

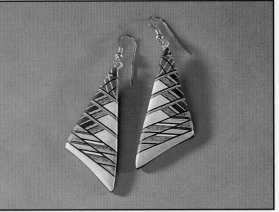

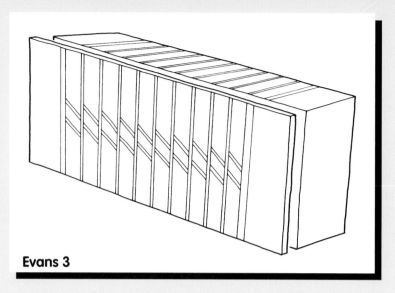

Evans 3

• Bandsaw 1/32" thick sections from the result (illustration **Evans 3**), and trim the edge of each section close to the chevron pattern.

• In illustration **Evans 4**, the line along which this trimming cut is made is drawn at a constant distance from the chevron pattern. To produce the slightly inverted-V form of the design in the photographs, however, this trimming cut should be made at a slight angle.

• Orient the trimmed chevron sections in mirror-image or bookmatch sequence, and reassemble atop a 1/8" thick substrate of solid contrasting wood. Draw the outline of the final piece in pencil and bandsaw. The result is illustrated in **Evans 5**.

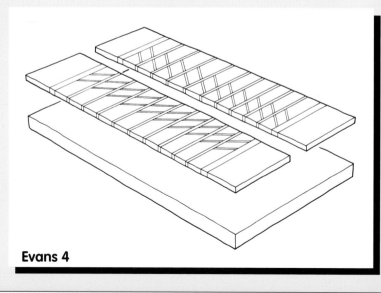

Evans 4

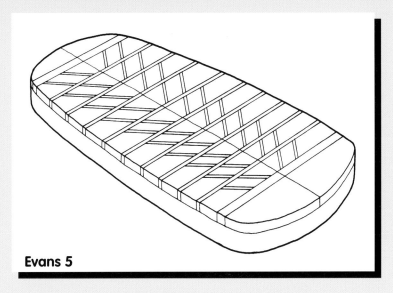

Evans 5

• Shape, sand, and polish the workpiece. Apply a hand-rubbed oil finish, wax, and buff, or spray with clear lacquer. Attach bolo tie fitting.
• The necklaces are made following the same procedures as the earrings, pendants, and bolos. Beads are milled from 1/4" square stock, drilled, shaped, and sanded.

BONNIE KLEIN

I turn for the love of the creative process," writes Bonnie Klein from her studio in Renton, Washington. "I am addicted to discovery, progress, and the fact that perfection is forever elusive. But as I strive for it, yesterday's challenges become the basic skills of tomorrow." Best known for turning miniatures, she also turns lidded containers, bowls, and many other small scale projects, such as replacement spindles for antique and furniture restorers.

Bonnie has travelled all over the United States, as well as to Canada, England, Ireland, and Australia, demonstrating her woodturning techniques and conducting workshops. "I love to travel, and to share my enthusiasm for turning with others. I especially enjoy working with young people, because I fear they are losing the opportunity to learn woodworking skills in school."

Her interest in sharing her knowledge and advancing the art of ornamental turning has led Bonnie to design and manufacture a specialized lathe for small turnings. She also produces a line of woodturning tools, and a lathe attachment for milling screw threads, as well as series of instructional videotapes.

• Turned on a lathe from rosewood and lignum vitae, the finger rings have an outside diameter of 7/8". For complete instructions on turnings of this type, please see the Sterling/Chappelle publication, *The Art of the Lathe* by Patrick Spielman.

• The baseball necklace is made from 42 miniature ebony baseball bats, each 3-3/8" long and 5/16" in diameter at the business end. They are strung with 1/4" diameter store-bought brass beads in the shape of baseballs.
• The bolo ties are turned from 1-5/8" ebony and pink ivorywood turning squares 3/8" thick.

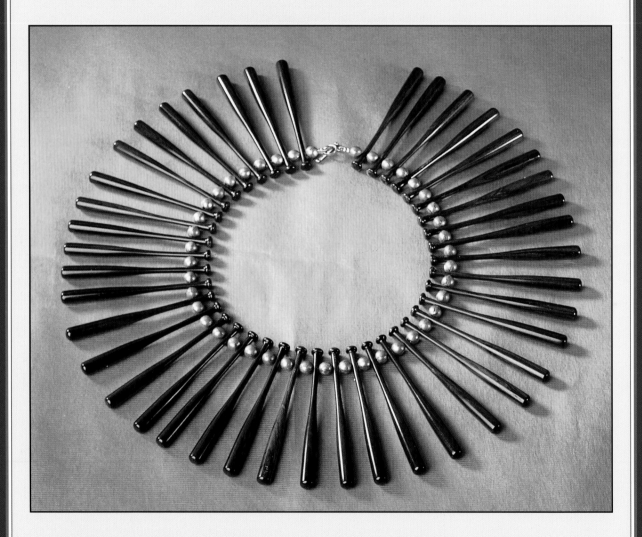

After turning the circular form, Bonnie details the surface with a patterned design called chatterwork or enginework.
• The 1" long cord-ends are turned from matching 3/8" square stock; drill a 1/8" diameter hole in each end for insertion of the braided tie cord. Attach a bolo tie backing.

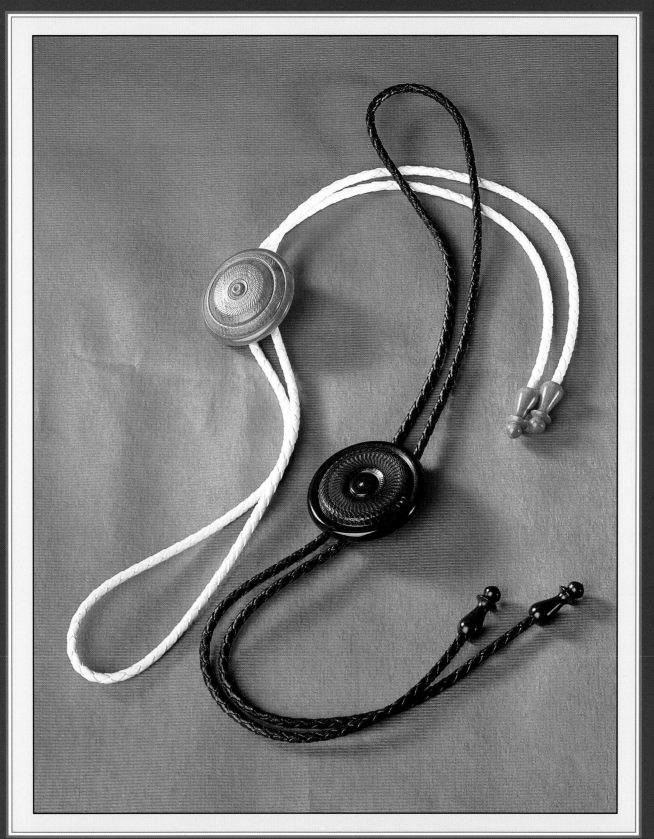

Photo by Dave Dornlas

CAROL
WINDSOR

Carol Windsor's interest in jewelry began during high school, when a buyer for a local department store asked where she got the earrings she was wearing. Carol had made them herself, and she was soon supplying the store with her work. Although her college major was in ceramics, she had taken a number of metals and jewelry courses, and when she needed a job, this led her back to making jewelry.

"I began to incorporate wood in my designs because it's such a great material to work with. Wood has a softness to it, even though it's also hard, and it's really warm – unlike metal, which is stiff and cold. Wood seems more human, perhaps because it was grown. Carving came naturally to me because of my ceramics training, and also because I'd done a lot of carving in wax, the first stage in lost-wax casting.

"I think of my work as a series of experiments. In the Landscape Pin (page 137), for example, I was exploring how to combine metal with wood. In the General Purpose Prod (page 134) and The Marriage Spoon (page 136), I'm trying to develop a vocabulary of tools that speak to the dilemmas we face in being human. The Marriage Spoon has two boats that are connected, but at the same time they're separate, suspended on opposite ends, even though they're part of the same tool.

"I carve the surface details like graffiti, or like the things that pass through your mind while you're doing something else. They are kind of symbols or reminders to me about personal imagery. The act of making them is spontaneous: they lack order, but that's what our lives are like."

• For the "Hand-Comb" earrings (page 134), cut the basic design from two ebony blocks, each 2" x 2" x 3/16", using the scroll saw. Embellish with a carved surface design, then polish.

• Carve the "Pod" earrings from 3/4" ebony cubes. Use a 1/32" drill bit to drill holes for silver wire. Glue short lengths of wire into each hole with epoxy; when dry, sand off the excess.

• Carve the "General Purpose Prod" from an ebony block 3/4" x 3/4" x 2-1/4". The silver cap that holds the point may be detailed with enamel.

• Scrollsaw and carve the brooch, "Comb or Cut.....A Tool for Entanglements", from a 1/4" x 2" x 3" piece of ebony.

• To make the pod-shaped brooch, bandsaw the rough shape from a block of ebony 3/4" x 3/4" x 3-1/2". Use a Dremel or other flexible shaft tool or carving knives to cut the central rift and radial scoring. Apply the red detailing with enamel and a small brush. The seven suture-like bands are short lengths of gold wire, anchored into 1/32" diameter holes drilled on the drill press.

Photo by Dawn Nelson

W I L L I A M
H A R R I S
&
D A W N
N E L S O N

Dawn Nelson and William Harris have perfected a style of mixed-media jewelry in which hardwoods are carved and constructed in combination with semiprecious stones, natural flowers, and insects, the latter carefully transformed into sterling silver through the process of lost-wax casting.

"William and I have the perfect collaboration," Dawn says about their artistic partnership. "William's the woodworker, and he does all his cutting by hand with a fine jeweler's saw. As he sits at his workbench, which he calls his altar – it's actually an antique Chinese altar table – the ideas for our jewelry pieces just go back and forth between us. It's becoming more and more difficult to distinguish who does what.

"We grew up in different states and trees. William was an apple in Michigan; I was a linden in New Jersey. But when we met in a bead store in Georgia, we recognized each other as spiritual family right away.

"Today, in our studio overlooking Lake Allatoona, the sky is a twenty-four hour extravaganza. While bumblebees visit, spiders raise families, toads sing, and lizards play freeze tag, we listen to tree stories, and turn what we experience into jewelry made from rare hardwoods, gemstones, and beads, and from natural plants and creatures transformed into precious metals, then adorned with symbols ancient and universal."

- Using a sketch pad, work out the basic design of the piece. On the bandsaw, mill stock for the wood components.
- Use the scrollsaw or hand-held jeweler's saw to cut out the shapes.
- Apply a hard-rubbed oil finish.
- Consult a library for instructional materials on lost-wax casting. No insects need be harmed in the process: Dawn Nelson and William Harris use only dead insects, often collected for them by sharp-eyed children.
- Drill 1/32" diameter holes for insertion of pearls, beads, and other stones that come with attached shafts.
- Screw in threaded rings for attaching chains.
- Assemble and attach pinbacks or other findings as needed.

- The wood components of these earrings, brooches, and necklaces are made from 1/16" to 1/8" blocks of ebony, purpleheart, pink ivory, tulipwood, cocobolo, and apple burl. The semiprecious stones include fresh- and salt-water pearls, garnet, blue lace agate, lapis, jade, amethyst, tourmaline, citrine, faceted quartz, carnelian, onyx, and serpentine, in addition to sterling silver chain and castings, and glass beads.

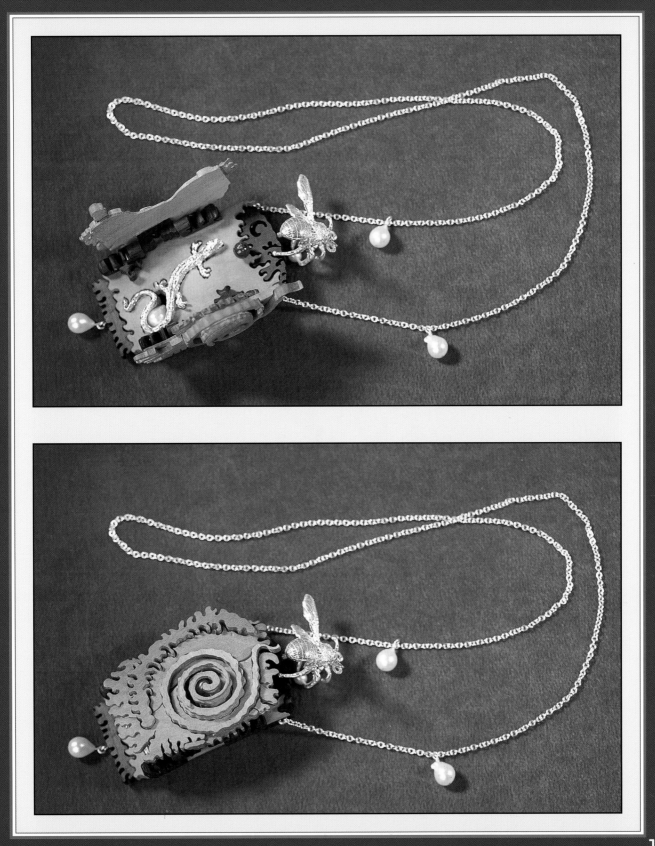

INCHES TO MILLIMETRES AND CENTIMETRES

MM-Millimetres   CM-Centimetres

INCHES	MM	CM	INCHES	CM	INCHES	CM
1/8	3	0.9	9	22.9	30	76.2
1/4	6	0.6	10	25.4	31	78.7
3/8	10	1.0	11	27.9	32	81.3
1/2	13	1.3	12	30.5	33	83.8
5/8	16	1.6	13	33.0	34	86.4
3/4	19	1.9	14	35.6	35	88.9
7/8	22	2.2	15	38.1	36	91.4
1	25	2.5	16	40.6	37	94.0
1 1/4	32	3.2	17	43.2	38	96.5
1 1/2	38	3.8	18	45.7	39	99.1
1 3/4	44	4.4	19	48.3	40	101.6
2	51	5.1	20	50.8	41	104.1
2 1/2	64	6.4	21	53.3	42	106.7
3	76	7.6	22	55.9	43	109.2
3 1/2	89	8.9	23	58.4	44	111.8
4	102	10.2	24	61.0	45	114.3
4 1/2	114	11.4	25	63.5	46	116.8
5	127	12.7	26	66.0	47	119.4
6	152	15.2	27	68.6	48	121.9
7	178	17.8	28	71.1	49	124.5
8	203	20.3	29	73.7	50	127.0

YARDS TO METRES

YARDS	METRES	YARDS	METRES	YARDS	METRES	YARDS	METRES	YARDS	METRES
1/8	0.11	2 1/8	1.94	4 1/8	3.77	6 1/8	5.60	8 1/8	7.43
1/4	0.23	2 1/4	2.06	4 1/4	3.89	6 1/4	5.72	8 1/4	7.54
3/8	0.34	2 3/8	2.17	4 3/8	4.00	6 3/8	5.83	8 3/8	7.66
1/2	0.46	2 1/2	2.29	4 1/2	4.11	6 1/2	5.94	8 1/2	7.77
5/8	0.57	2 5/8	2.40	4 5/8	4.23	6 5/8	6.06	8 5/8	7.89
3/4	0.69	2 3/4	2.51	4 3/4	4.34	6 3/4	6.17	8 3/4	8.00
7/8	0.80	2 7/8	2.63	4 7/8	4.46	6 7/8	6.29	8 7/8	8.12
1	0.91	3	2.74	5	4.57	7	6.40	9	8.23
1 1/8	1.03	3 1/8	2.86	5 1/8	4.69	7 1/8	6.52	9 1/8	8.34
1 1/4	1.14	3 1/4	2.97	5 1/4	4.80	7 1/4	6.63	9 1/4	8.46
1 3/8	1.26	3 3/8	3.09	5 3/8	4.91	7 3/8	6.74	9 3/8	8.57
1 1/2	1.37	3 1/2	3.20	5 1/2	5.03	7 1/2	6.86	9 1/2	8.69
1 5/8	1.49	3 5/8	3.31	5 5/8	5.14	7 5/8	6.97	9 5/8	8.80
1 3/4	1.60	3 3/4	3.43	5 3/4	5.26	7 3/4	7.09	9 3/4	8.92
1 7/8	1.71	3 7/8	3.54	5 7/8	5.37	7 7/8	7.20	9 7/8	9.03
2	1.83	4	3.66	6	5.49	8	7.32	10	9.14